"Sruti Ram and I were friends for over forty-five years. He was an intrepid explorer of inner realities and a dedicated miner for a heart of gold. This book is the story of the unfolding of his path to the One." —**Krishna Das, Kirtan singer, composer, and musician; author of** *Flow of Grace: Chanting the Hanuman Chalisa* **and** *Chants of a Lifetime: Searching for a Heart of Gold*

"Sruti Ram was a true Bhakta with a wide-open heart. His essence comes through loud and clear in *All Roads Lead to Ram*." —**Daniel Goleman, author of** *Emotional Intelligence: Why It Can Matter More Than IQ*

"Sruti Ram was a fearless adventurer—a believer in miracles, mysticism, and magic. His wondrous life proves that for the sincere seeker, the one who cultivates the highest intention, all roads lead to God, eventually but inevitably." —**Sharon Gannon, cofounder of Jivamukti Yoga; author of** *Jivamukti Yoga: Practices for Liberating Body and Soul*

"Sruti Ram was my neighbor in our little Catskill Mountain town, a meditation teacher at the retreat center I cofounded, a chant leader, a free-flowing fountain of wisdom—and sometimes, the person who cut my hair. He was somehow able to weave the threads of his diverse roles and many talents into one tapestry named Sruti Ram. He always insisted that there was actually no such person as Sruti Ram, no such thing as time, no such thing as death. There was only love. Sometimes when I would run into him in the grocery store, he'd be standing there in front of the produce—with his classy eyeglasses and colorful scarf—just standing there, in love with the vegetables, radiating devotional gratitude to all the beings who grew and harvested and transported and displayed God's bounty. He was Bhakti—devotion—incarnate. We lost him too soon, but he left us this book, a rousing collection of stories and nuggets of wisdom from his beautiful life." —**Elizabeth Lesser, cofounder of Omega Institute; author of** *Broken Open: How Difficult Times Can Help Us Grow* **and** *Cassandra Speaks: When Women Are the Storytellers, the Human Story Changes*

"Sruti Ram reveals the road less traveled and the life of commitment to the journey within. One feels the unfolding of life's magic that arises not from mental planning but rather from trusting the heart to show the way of true happiness in life. I admire Sruti Ram's devotion to follow a spiritual path as an authentic way of life in a society focused too much on material concerns." —**Stephan Rechtschaffen, MD, founder of Blue Spirit Costa Rica and cofounder of Omega Institute**

"This is a lovely, deeply engaging book! Sruti Ram shares, with elegant grace, the evolution of his own journey to India and, ultimately, into the Heart of God. His quest began with a deep inner yearning felt by so many of us growing up in the West in the late 1960s and early 1970s. We sensed that the most effective paths for responding to that yearning were known and practiced in India. Sruti Ram's book takes us to the origins of the yoga revolution that has now spread far and wide in our culture. It reveals—in a beautifully warm, accessible style—how one lovely man found what we are all seeking. That inner journey often involved traveling 12,000 miles and immersing ourselves in the sacred, ancient practices of Mother India. This is the story of what it was like to find yoga, meditation, and spirituality decades before there were yoga studios and classes on every corner. The ironic realization is that, ultimately, the Path we are all seeking lies not in some exotic land—or even in the local yoga center. The journey 'hOMe' begins and unfolds within each and every one of us as we transition from living in our judging minds to living in our compassionate Heart through Love, sincere practice, and Devotion. Namaste." —**Ramananda John E. Welshons, author of** *One Soul, One Love, One Heart: The Sacred Path to Healing All Relationships, When Prayers Aren't Answered,* **and** *Awakening from Grief*

All Roads Lead to *Ram*

THE PERSONAL HISTORY
of a
SPIRITUAL ADVENTURER

SRUTI RAM

Monkfish Book Publishing Company
Rhinebeck, New York

Paperback ISBN 978-1-948626-33-0
eBook ISBN 978-1-948626-34-7

Registration number TXu 2-074-360

Library of Congress Cataloging-in-Publication Data

Names: Ram, Sruti, 1943- author.
Title: All roads lead to ram : the personal history of a spiritual
   adventurer / Sruti Ram.
Description: Rhinebeck, New York : Monkfish Book Publishing Company, 2021.
Identifiers: LCCN 2021007471 (print) | LCCN 2021007472 (ebook) | ISBN
   9781948626330 (paperback) | ISBN 9781948626347 (ebook)
Subjects: LCSH: Hindus--Biography. | Ram, Sruti, 1943---Teachings.
Classification: LCC BL1175.R21845 A3 2021 (print) | LCC BL1175.R21845
   (ebook) | DDC 294.5092 [B]--dcundefined
LC record available at https://lccn.loc.gov/2021007471
LC ebook record available at https://lccn.loc.gov/2021007472

Interior and cover design by Colin Rolfe
Front cover photo by Chaithanya Krishnan/Getty Images

Monkfish Book Publishing Company
22 East Market Street, Suite 304
Rhinebeck, NY 12572
(845) 876-4861
monkfishpublishing.com

To my Beloved Guru, Sri Sri Sri Neem Karoli Baba
And to my brilliant mentor, Baba Ram Dass

There were many of us making the trip to the East.
Each one of our stories is an adventure in itself.
We all pursued the particular yoga
that our karmas dictated.
Here is one of our stories.
It leads us from a deep yearning heart to
a spiritual manifestation of bhakti,
the way of the heart.

RAM DASS

CONTENTS

REMEMBRANCES

BEYOND TIME

I WAS SRUTI Ram's next-door neighbor. When he found out I was a writer and an editor, he said, "Well, now I know why you're here." He called it an obvious example of the universe aligning in infinite correlation—even though, as I told him, my house was the only rental that would take my dogs and me after a hellacious breakup. *Okay*, he said, in that way he had of not acquiescing at all, just agreeing for the sake of it.

Sruti Ram was certainly a man of paradoxes. He could be testy and impatient and open-heartedly loving, nearly in the same breath. His intense focus while singing or practicing was offset by his total goofy joy when greeting my dogs, who'd race over to his house for a dose of him whenever they could. He mixed Costco pajamas with very stylish woodgrain eyeglasses. Whenever I went to the city, I'd always ask what he wanted from there. He never wanted me to go to any trouble, *except* if I could find a very rare holiday cake that was only available at Dean & DeLuca one week out of the year. Of course, I combed the city until I found the one store that still had it. He devoured the whole thing in four days, then swore he needed to do a fast. All of these qualities seemed to be equal parts of someone very alive and rare and in love with life.

But there was one true contradiction in Sruti Ram, and it revolved around time. We were working on this book, a narrative of the singular arc of his life, yet he believed—or believes—in the timelessness of the divine. He had been writing the manuscript for years but wanted help fleshing out and organizing all the stories. The book needs *something*, he said. Ordinarily so articulate, he couldn't put this *something* into words. But the book was his baby, and he wanted the best for it.

So, I'd cross the enchanted meadow from my house to his, passing the shrines in his yard, the songbirds at his feeders. We'd sit in his living room, his crystals and prisms sparkling and dancing. Chapter by chapter, I'd ask him, "When *was* this?"

"When I was in India," he'd say.

"When?"

"Does it matter?"

"Let's anchor it in time," I'd say.

"Time doesn't matter," he'd say. "There *is* no time."

I'd insist that it did matter because he wanted to tell the story of his life and his spiritual search, and such stories can't resolve without a beginning and an end.

"Fine," he'd say. "It was years ago."

"When?"

"I don't know. Nineteen ninety, okay? Is that good enough?"

But I had to order the events of his life somehow, so I'd keep asking: "Did that come before the magical visitation on the golden throne or after?"

He'd look at me.

Again, and again, we did that two-step. (We had help too, from the skillful Nina Shengold.) And when we were all done, he was grateful. By giving the stories an order, he saw for the first time the full measure of all he'd done. "What a life," he said. "Wow. But remember, we're only doing this whole chronological business for the sake of telling my story. Time means nothing. There are no beginnings, no endings. There is only love."

Now we are left mourning an ending none of us wanted and no one could have predicted. I think Sruti Ram had inklings, though. His body was wearing down. He dreaded catching the coronavirus because his life force wasn't quite what it had been. He was feeling his physical age, and I think, too, the weight of recent losses—Ram Dass and his own brother among them—so he was having to reckon with time despite his beliefs. And the fact that this amazing, anointed, astonishing being was taken away in the worst of ways is a tragedy which all of us who knew him are reeling from.

In the end, Sruti Ram ran out of time—at least in this life. But as he would correct me, his *body* ran out, not him. He simply cast off his shell. Sruti Ram was and still is a perfect being: infinite, beyond time, loving us all, reminding us of the divine in the snow, in the sun, in each other. I truly think that's the way he wants us to know his story, and that's the way he lives on in us all.

—JANA MARTIN

PREFACE

It's my hope that these stories are inspirational and enhance the teachings contained within them. Many have an interest in how these phenomenal experiences have affected my life personally. In these chapters, I would like to share more of the effects of devotional love—and the wonder that manifests from that powerful energy.

Through the grace of my guru, I will attempt to convey my process along the devotional path. I was fortunate to have the guidance of many fine teachers and joyful *bhaktas* for this journey.

It is so very important to recognize that extraordinary things can and do happen. My guidelines have been, and continue to be:

Support the Dharma.

Keep love in your heart.

Have as much fun as you can.

OM SRI SRI SRI SAT GURU NEEM KAROLI BABA KI JAI

But gradually, I became disenchanted with the organization of religion and the lack of universal unity contained within the religious dogma. The Catholic Church made me feel that we [Christians] were totally different from everyone else. But I always knew we were all one. I was too young to know how to put this into words, but I deeply believed that we were all the same. I didn't experience the differences in race, dogmas, and beliefs. I just knew that we all really believed in the same thing beneath all of our cultural variations.

And then, at the age of thirteen, my hormones kicked in, and my father died. With his death, I was cast into the role of the man of the house, which was not a role I really wanted. I missed him profoundly, every day. He had been a strong and demonstrative person, and I knew that he loved me with his whole heart. I felt abandoned, and this feeling would plague me for most of my adult life. But worst of all, my angels disappeared. I just went to bed one night, and they were gone.

My new role as a responsible personality in the house who was suddenly without his lifelong friends, the angels, was a confounding situation for me. I had no male role model and felt confused and vulnerable. Though I had an older brother, he was off on his own personal journey and was unavailable to me. With my hormones raging

Sruti Ram and his Aunt Flo after his First Communion.

and my life changing, the outside world began to creep into my consciousness.

Now I filled my time with music and art. Fortunately, I had an exceptional mother who was capable and smart enough to provide a life for us that was comfortable and secure. When I was old enough, I got a car for my birthday.

Now I could travel. I could expand my horizons. Having a car gave me the luxury of lots of new friends and experiences. I even studied opera for a time, and I loved the portal to the more esoteric side that music provided. I became interested in singing rock 'n' roll, and being part of our group was a joyful time in my young adulthood.

I also became a hairdresser—and I was really good at it. To my amazement, this occupation brought in lots of money, and it introduced me to the whole new world of style and fashion. It was a glamorous time, filled with music and affluence, and I had a blast seeking out fun and worldly exposure. It was a playground—and I thought I was a player. Little did I know.

CHAPTER 1

THE FIRST TIME

IT WAS 1968. I was twenty-five years old and living in a very comfortable home in New York City. By all standards, I should have been happy with my life, which had just about everything the world could offer. I was young, successful, popular, and healthy. But I wasn't really happy or contented.

Several friends had told me about Yogi Dinkar, an old friend of Maharishi Mahesh Yogi, who was giving out mantras—for a price, of course. Getting a mantra was all the rage since the Beatles had planted it into our young minds. I made an appointment to visit the mantra man. He lived and taught in a small studio on Fifty-Seventh Street in Manhattan.

I arrived at the appointed time and found a rather strange old man dressed in Indian clothes. There were many people taking hatha yoga classes from him and others sitting around his makeshift waiting room wanting to receive a mantra. I took my place and waited with the others. We were an average-looking bunch and waited with high expectations for our turn with the old fellow.

He was really quite a character. He seemed to be about seventy and was in pretty good shape, being a hatha yoga teacher and all. One of his most unexpected characteristics was his thick Jewish

Sruti Ram as a young man.

accent. He was very animated and rather loud. He certainly did not fit the model I had for a yogi.

Finally, it was my turn. He called me to his desk, and we sat quietly for a moment. He looked deeply into my eyes, which was not what I had observed happening with the others, and said loudly in front of all, "So, you vant a mantra?"

"Why, yes, that's correct."

"Vell, not for you, not now."

"Why not?" I asked. "I have my appointment with you and the hundred dollars. Why can't I get one now?"

"You're not ready for it yet."

I was shocked to be singled out from the others and rejected in this way. At first, I was intimidated. Then it quickly morphed to anger.

"Well, when can I get one?"

"You have to do hatha yoga for a while before I'll give it to you."

Oh, *rats*. He wants me to invest in some classes, I thought. He's just another money-hungry old man, capitalizing on a new vogue.

But I really wanted a mantra. It was so cool to have a mantra, and all my friends expected me to return with one. Damn, I was really mad. But I agreed to take a class. I started going every day after work, thinking I could rush the process along and get the damn mantra from him.

After two weeks of classes, I asked again, "Can I have the mantra now?"

He had transformed a small closet with lots of pictures of Indian deities and various accoutrements. A person would enter that sacred space with him and emerge about fifteen minutes later, all smiles and happy with his or her accomplishment. During the previous two weeks, many people had gone into the special little room with

Lord Ram. This was the first image of him that Sruti Ram received from Yogi Dinkar.

Then, on one occasion, he turned to me and said, "I'm going back to India to live."

He told me that he wanted me to come to India and live there with him. I was crushed to think of being without him. But now I really flipped out. "No," I replied, "I don't want to live in India! I live here and have a life here. I shall miss you terribly, but I just can't go with you. What will I do without you, without your guidance and knowledge? How can you go and leave me here like this?"

He said that I really should go with him. But, he added, he understood—and would always remember me in his prayers.

Seeing the look of disappointment and fear on my face, he grew silent. After a moment, he said that a new teacher would find me and that all would be taken care of. He assured me that I had been an excellent student, and that my sense of devotion to the teacher would manifest toward another very quickly.

He moved very fast after that. He was gone in a matter of three weeks. I never saw or heard from him again. But I never lost the memory of the funny Jewish man in Indian clothes who changed the course of my life. He introduced me to a form of the Divine that would forever be in my awareness.

The young Sruti Ram.

It actually was a classic guru/devotee lesson, although I did not know it then. However, as time went on, my knowledge of the Indian traditions deepened, and I heard many tales of how teachers would prepare a serious student for a profound spiritual event in their lives just as he did for me.

I believe that the dear old yogi cultivated trust and made the devotional aspect so much more valuable to me. He also educated me in the ways of the Indian culture through hatha yoga, as well as his teachings, his philosophy, and his very presence.

Looking back, it's now obvious to me how Yogi Dinkar made the mantra and its meaning in my existence much more desirable. Consequently, the wisdom became larger and more intensely significant. The great lesson was to acknowledge the internal changes that were planted and nurtured by his careful and deliberate teachings.

When we are in the fire of purification, only the impurities burn. We just have to do our part of the program. So, open the door and walk in. The rest happens on autopilot, like it or not.

CHAPTER 2

OUT OF THE BLUE: THE UPSTATE SWAMI

FOR SOME TIME after my experience with Yogi Dinkar, I would think about India. I assured myself that I would probably never go there. It was so far away and totally foreign to my life and culture. I had no idea how important his counsel—that I would find another teacher and would someday go to India —would be in my life.

In the meantime, I continued to live my normal life in New York City. But I missed Yogi Dinkar and was losing interest in my usual activities, in just having a good time in the city with my friends. Instead, I found myself hungry for more knowledge of Indian culture and the practices of devotees. Without a teacher, I continued to read volumes of books on the subject, consumed with a desire to delve deeper into my meditation. What a profound effect Yogi Dinkar's magic closet had set in motion!

I continued to meditate, using the mantra and the picture of Lord Ramachandra, with his lovely, androgynous look and long hair and earrings, holding a bow and arrow. When I meditated, I used the mantra—*Ram*—and the picture, before closing my eyes.

And little by little, my world changed. I became much more aware of the desires and needs of my old life. How superficial all of that was! It produced no real sense of joyfulness or development of a higher consciousness. That's what I wanted: to develop more of a connection with the higher power that had infiltrated my being when I was with Yogi Dinkar.

I had changed, but my world had not kept up with my spiritual evolution. Then two good friends of mine got a house in the country, a peaceful house in a natural, rustic environment. I went to stay with them and ended up sharing their house for many years. It was a lovely home, just an hour from the city. My friends had developed their own mild curiosity about meditation and were supportive of my new infatuation. Life was good there. But still, there was no actual resource for my metaphysical hunger. The isolation was both wonderful and terrible.

I started teaching hatha yoga, which enabled me to acquire new friends and encouraged me to continue my practice. I started a meditation collective, and more and more people came. One of my neighbors, whose house was within walking distance from mine, seemed to have the same type of desire for spiritual development, so we created a weekly gathering at her home. We studied *A Course in Miracles,* which proved to be good for our mutual craving for more spirituality in our lives. But I still craved more powerful teaching—I needed more spiritual potency.

But my friends, who had also received mantras from Yogi Dinkar, were not nearly as changed as I seemed to be. They didn't seem to have any of the life-altering effects, inwardly or otherwise, that I did. And I was becoming more and more interested in the different methods of meditation and teachers. But no one really seemed like a good replacement for Yogi Dinkar. None of them had his intensity.

It was quite unsettling. Over that year, I became more and more introspective and contemplative, searching within myself and questioning everything. But I felt even more discontent than I had before. All my friends thought I had gone off the deep end, and my two housemates were genuinely concerned about me. They loved me deeply, they told me, but it seemed to them that all the meditation and practice I was doing was ultimately making me unhappier. And I was, truly, getting more confused: What the heck was I doing in the middle of nowhere? How would I ever find a teacher out here? But I couldn't go back to the city. I couldn't bear the social demands of the city. I was really in crisis. I doubted my practice. I doubted the old man. I doubted God.

Nothing gave me comfort.

It was a gloomy morning in the dead of winter, a typical dank and cold upstate New York winter morning. I was miserable. I had invested so much time and energy in making a new life in the country. But once again, my efforts seemed fruitless and unfulfilling. It seemed there was no one who could relate to my predicament. My moods would sink, and there seemed to be no place to seek refuge, no oasis where I could recover, regenerate, or find some of the joy I'd had in the presence and guidance of a teacher. I felt utterly alone.

I decided I'd take my tormented psyche and go for a walk in the woods. I walked and walked, my despair building up. I wound up sitting on a rock somewhere among the bare trees, overwhelmed with despair. I began to cry: "Oh, Lord, please give me a sign. *Anything* to help confirm I'm on the right track." There I was, in the cold and lonely woods, and I was afraid I was on the verge of a breakdown.

I don't know how long I sat there, but I was getting chilled and wet, so I decided it was time to go back to the house. I got off the rock and started walking back. And far ahead of me, off in the distance among the trees, I noticed something: a flash of orange, a glimpse of bright color. It was so vivid and out of place in the winter woods. What was it? It fascinated me. I found myself heading towards it, drawn to it, as if called by an almost magical force.

I continued to walk towards it. The closer I got, the larger and brighter the area of color became. I finally reached it. And lo and behold, it was a man. It was a little Indian man, dressed head to toe in flame orange cloth. He was carrying a wooden walking stick, its bottom tip wrapped in a plastic Wonder Bread wrapper to keep it dry.

An Indian *swami*.

An Indian swami in the woods, here in upstate New York.

What was going on?

Standing there above me on a rock ledge, resplendent in his orange robes, he was beautiful. I was sure I was imagining the entire thing. But I wasn't.

There we stood, in the middle of the woods, looking at each other in silence. A few minutes went by. I could feel some kind of energy pulsating through my body. My heart was pumping, my pulse racing.

Was this my sign?

I introduced myself. "I'm George," I said.

He said his name was Swami Swaanandashram.

And just how had he come to be in the woods that day?

He told me he was visiting one of my neighbors for a few weeks and had decided to go for a walk in the woods.

I don't remember what I said in response. But I do remember that I had the unmistakable feeling of being in an incredible presence. This man, clad in orange, seemed to have the ability to see deep inside of me, as though he was looking directly into my heart. At least that's how it felt out there in the winter woods. And it felt as if God had heard my plea. The time being right, *wham!* There he was. He invited me to have some tea with him that very afternoon.

In the face of negative situations, have faith in the presence of a power stronger than you. You never know where it's going to appear. And when it does, listen to what it has to say. Listen with your heart.

CHAPTER 3

A SAPPHIRE RING

To this day I know that my yearning to find a teacher, so strong in my psyche, had overcome my own doubting mind and allowed a miracle to manifest itself. Swami Swaanandashram turned out to be a very learned and orthodox swami from the Shankaracharya sect, in which he held an elevated position. He was also a lawyer and an astrologer. We came to be close friends, and eventually, he took me on as a student. He was a brilliant teacher, with vast and powerful knowledge.

The Swami taught me about controlling my breath and chanting. Through his tutelage, I learned how to make my mind more of a servant and less of a master. By controlling the breath and using mantra as he prescribed it, my mind became much more disciplined. I felt less controlled by my emotions. It was an amazing development for me, learning all about the benefits of breath control and becoming the captain of the ship, so to speak. It was thrilling and exhilarating.

But that wasn't all he had to teach me. He taught me the power of gemstones—how wearing a certain stone could heal and change one's physical state. I had always been drawn to gems, so this was a fascinating new aspect of my mystical education, and I looked forward to when I could apply this knowledge to other people as well. But first I had a profound lesson to learn.

The Swami wore a strikingly beautiful sapphire ring. It had a huge stone, particularly magnificent. To my surprise, he offered it to me, but on one condition. I was to wear the ring for three days, and not take it off, even when I slept. After three days, I was to report to him about my dreams. Excitedly, I accepted the ring, more than eager to obey his demand. Piece of cake, I thought.

Not really: I wore the ring for three days and nights, keeping notes of my dreams. They were horrible dreams. As I reported to him, I'd been plagued with nightmares for those three nights, and on top of feeling exhausted, I felt completely ill. I regretted telling him this, as if I'd have let him down. But instead, he laughed. The reason I'd had such an awful time, he explained, was that the stone was too big for me. It wasn't a good stone for me. And as he continued, he knew I'd coveted the stone, and he wanted to fulfill that desire. But given my experiences over the past few days, it clearly wasn't right for me. And one thing about gems, he made it clear, is that it's crucial to understand how to use them.

I returned the ring.

When he was not engaged in conversation or study, the Swami was constantly chanting. *Hari Om*, he'd chant, *Hari Om*. He sang these sacred words with a beautiful melody. It was an intoxicating sound, filling his house whenever I came to see him. And it made my awareness of his communion with divinity even more pronounced—a natural part of his being.

I learned so much from him. He did my astrological life chart in the Indian manner, and was thrilled with my planets, their positions, and the timings of various transits. He interpreted my whole life according to his astrological computations—what my real work would be, even the date of my death. We had many talks about what he saw there. He explained that I had a direct connection to Lord Rama, a revelation that jolted me: I had never told him of the RAM mantra given to me by Yogi Dinkar, or of my meditation with the picture of Lord Ramachandra. But there it was.

He also gave me a Hindu name. This was a common practice, and I accepted it gratefully. He called me *Som Dev*—the deity of the moon. "Use this name until you're fifty years old," he told me, "and then change it to another name." I didn't know why, but all of this was fabulous—I was thrilled and delighted to be under his wing. Of course, I said. I'd do anything. Indeed, to do anything for this remarkable man was a great honor. He was one of the most devout men I have ever known.

While I was with him, he wrote several small books and in some he documented experiences I had with him. One such story, all true, went like this:

On the night the Swami was flying to California, I was sitting, meditating, at home. My friend Gail called to tell me that the Swami was taking the same flight as he was, and that he was on his way. I meditated again, and then headed to bed. Just a normal night. I went to sleep, and then suddenly, I was awake, very clear-headed. I heard him chanting, as if he was on a recording softly playing, though nothing was on. And in a flash, I felt as though I were sitting on the plane, right next to him.

He turned to me and smiled, and my body became filled with some new strange energy, like electricity. Then it stopped. A few seconds later it happened again, and then again, it stopped. The third time, this amazing sensation stayed with me for some fifteen minutes. I could see only a bright light—the brightest light I had ever witnessed at the time. It was powerful, mystical, and incredibly profound.

I knew then that he was always with me. That knowledge created a joy within me that served as my deliverance from the mundane existence I'd previously rejected. *This is it*, I thought. I shall be with him forever. The attachment would grow, and grow, and grow.

But of course, our time together would come to an end. He announced he was returning to India, and as Yogi Dinkar had, he suggested I visit him. He'd take care of my needs there, he said. I wouldn't have to worry about a thing. But I was still not ready to go to India. I could not bring myself to leave the United States. And I assumed he would return. I assumed I'd see him again.

I rode with him to the airport. I was sad, but he was fine with it all: so accepting and unattached to everything in this world, and yet so sweet. The thing about him was that decades before, he had spent seventeen years in an ice cave at the source of the Ganges, living on mantra, water, and salt. That kind of existence forges a disciplined sense of detachment. And it had certainly made him frail. I hadn't talked about it with him that much, but on that last car ride, I questioned him. "I've always wanted to know," I said. "Why would you abuse your body in that way for so many years? You have ruined your health."

"Yes, that is true, Som Dev," he said. "There were hardships to endure. But, oh, the visions—they were beyond explanation!"

We said our goodbyes and I escorted him to the gate. I bowed to him in the customary way, showing respect and admiration. Quietly we stood there in the airport. Then he inscribed his prayerbook and handed it me. "Use it when you do your rituals," he said.

This was curious. At that time, I did not perform any rituals. But I took it from him gratefully and told him that I would cherish it always.

Then he removed his shawl, part of that bright orange garment I'd seen glowing that day in the woods. It was beautifully embroidered in the Kashmiri style. As he placed it around my shoulders, a jolt of electrical energy ran through my body, and I burst into tears.

He put his hands on my shoulders and looked lovingly into my eyes. His look was one I understood. It was one I had come to recognize as a major event in the course of the teacher/student spiritual relationship: a giving, a letting go.

"Wear this when you teach," he said.

I hadn't planned on teaching. "Swami, when and what shall I teach?" I said.

"The time will present itself to you," he said. "You have done well. Have no fear, Som Dev. Ram is always with you."

And then he got on the plane, and once again, my beloved teacher was gone.

I was so blessed by that dear soul, so empowered by his teachings. There were so many lessons, including learning how to stabilize the power of faith in my heart, even when my mind was screaming with doubts. Look at what happened just when I needed it the most: On a winter's day in the woods, when I felt as despondent as the cold ground, convinced I'd never find a teacher, there he was.

Another lesson, though, was that a true teacher has the qualities of a saint, including no need for attachments. When the Swami left me behind, it was without any regret or hesitation. Yet I knew without question that he loved me, his student, deeply. The great teachers are attached to nothing: no fancy gems, no beautiful embroidered shawls, no devoted disciples, not even a personal prayer book. Nothing meant more to Swami Swaanandashram than his own relationship with the Divine, and the conditions that secured him in that actuality.

For a few years after his departure, he wrote to me occasionally. I always wrote back. But my letters came back unopened, marked "person unknown." Over the years since then I have been to India many times, and searched for information about him. But strangely, no one has ever heard of him. No one knew anything about this magical swami who was the *yogiraj* of the Shankaracharya sect. Yet I still have his letters, and they are very dear to me. So, who, I wonder, was that masked man?

What I do know is that he left me full of love, and a new understanding of the mystical tangents of spirituality. He helped me become a firm believer in the miracles of life that surround us and are available to us if we allow them to be. He enabled me to access these gifts. His delightful demeanor and countenance enlightened me as to the dynamic of a reliable and positive teacher. And he enriched my life with the ability to love my process and understand that all things come to us, the practitioners, who dedicate our intention to the devotional love of God. We must have a burning desire

Young Sruti Ram wearing Swami Swaanandashram's orange shawl.

for that illumination and press on in the face of doubt and confusion. That's why the work is referred to as a practice. As my friend Ram Dass once told me, "We are all just walking each other home."

Being a teacher is the ultimate service to humanity, and the best way to teach is to be. Swami was the perfect example of that philosophy: impeccable in his teachings, entirely dedicated to the service of others in his life. And indeed, it was he who taught me how to discipline the mind and control the breath, powerful techniques that have proved to be invaluable to my evolution. He may have been short in physical stature, but he left an indelible imprint on my psyche. In power and fortitude, he was a giant.

CHAPTER 4

INDIA CALLING

I HEARD ABOUT a woman yogi in the city who held *satsang*, spiritual meetings, once a week. Her name was Hilda. She was then a middle-aged woman who dressed in the Indian style and had lived in India as a young woman for almost two decades. She had studied with several teachers and had many wonderful experiences and stories to share. Her personality was warm and generous, with a motherly attitude towards everybody, no matter what his or her age. We would sing Indian devotional songs and, when the energy felt right, she would read and give commentary on the teachings she had lived by. I was delighted to find this group and continued to attend the meetings regularly for about a year.

During this time, I consumed books about the masters and their journeys, including one of Hilda's favorites—an

Hilda Charlton.

Indian saint named Sathya Sai Baba. There were many tales about his miracles and wondrous events that were so phenomenal I just couldn't believe them. Though doubtful, I must admit I was totally curious. I had to see it myself to believe it all. I also had been reading about an Indian mystic who was reported to be a direct incarnation of God.

Many folks were inspired to travel to India through Hilda's loving influence and fabulous stories. Finally, I came to the conclusion that I was ready to go to India. I started to make inquiries as to who would travel with me. At that time, no one was willing to go and, no matter who I asked, there was some obstacle that appeared. I even asked all my nonspiritual friends and absolutely no one wanted to accompany me to India. At first, I felt disheartened, but eventually I elected to go alone. I made all the arrangements, gleaned all the information that I could from the *sangha,* and left for an unknown adventure.

I arrived in Bombay scared, confused, and questioning my reasons for going it alone. I remember standing at the airport door looking out into the mass confusion of a Bombay street. There were cars, animals, thousands of people, and a symphony of new smells and colors. I took a friend's advice and went directly to a luxury hotel and holed up there for a few days. The theory was to slowly venture out and taste the culture, thus adapting to the changes gradually and gently.

Every day, I would explore some of the city's avenues and then retreat back to safety and comfort. After a few days of seeing the abject poverty and a lifestyle that was so completely the opposite of everything I had ever known, I became very sad and lonely and was deeply concerned that I had made a huge mistake.

What am I doing here? I thought. I wondered if I would ever be able to get around, much less find this Sai Baba. One evening in my hotel room, where I had set up a small altar with a picture of Sai Baba, I tearfully spoke to that picture and pleaded for help. I begged him to get me to his refuge.

The very next morning, as I found my way back to the familiar restaurant in the hotel and was having my breakfast at the counter, I happened to look at the gentleman sitting next to me. Much to my delight, I noticed that he was wearing a ring with a picture of Sai Baba on it. I immediately started a conversation with him.

He was very friendly and a fountain of information. He told me about a man who lived in Bombay who could help me with all my plans. Consequently, I called the man, who invited me to his home for tea. It turned out that he was a wealthy devotee of Sai Baba and very influential within that scene. He invited me to be his guest on his private plane and that he would personally get me in to see Sai Baba. This would all take place within about ten days' time. I couldn't accept as true the level of my good fortune. Was this in fact a miracle? Delighted, I returned to the hotel, filled with peace that all would be well and that I would accomplish my quest.

During that ten-day waiting period, I became quite brave and comfortable with being in this strange and fascinating place. I also had the occasion to meet some other hotel guests—two very wealthy antique collectors from Italy who invited me to accompany them on their daily buying jaunts. It was great fun and very educational. I got to be very at ease with them and their European ways.

The lifestyle they enjoyed was very impressive and they were more than willing to share it with me. The day came that these men were going to leave Bombay and continue on to Goa. It was a few days before I was due to go to Baba's *ashram*. I met my new friends on the morning of their departure and wished them a farewell. "Oh," they said, "we don't want you to say goodbye. We want you to come with us." They both overwhelmed me with their petitions to join them. They were going to see fabulous things and have more fun than could even be described, and I knew it. They were relentless. And they convinced me. In a flash, I made a decision. I ran up to my room, packed my things, checked out of the hotel, and jumped into their limo. Just before leaving, I called the Indian gentleman who had been so kind about making arrangements for me to see Sai Baba. I told him that I was going to delay my arrival at Baba's ashram.

We got on a plane. In an hour I was in Goa at the Hotel Mandovi. My head was spinning. I could not believe that I had forgone all my existing plans to meet God—the very plans that assured me a privileged arrival and the care that I craved so deeply. What had I done?

The time in Goa with the two Italians was great fun, of course. It was an exceptional experience. But still, I could not come to grips with the fact that I had just turned and run from the dream that had brought me to India.

Our time together was short, about two weeks, before they left India and returned to Europe. By then I was quite the traveler and had no fear about continuing on my own. I made arrangements to travel on the deluxe bus to central India. What a joke! The deluxe bus was in shambles. It had broken windows, broken seats, no heat, and took nineteen hours to get to my destination. Literally, it was a nightmare. Wild monkeys plagued us. As if that wasn't enough, people brought animals on the bus. I went to sleep on the floor of the bus with a goat.

Finally, we arrived at Bangalore. I had gotten the name of a *bhavan* that catered to Sai Baba devotees and I was greeted nicely and given a safe space.

The schedule to actually see Sai Baba was posted and, to my delight, the opportunity to have the visitation was on the next day. Early that morning I hired a rickshaw to take me to the ashram where he lived. I was directed into the courtyard to await his arrival.

In those days, there were merely a couple of hundred people present for *darshan* (years later there were never less than five thousand). Darshan was the privilege of actually being in his presence. I stood there patiently. I had been told that if I wrote a note and held it in my hand, there was a chance that he would take it from me. If he did, it would be a sign of recognition. I composed a short note: "Dear Baba, my HEART is open to you."

We all waited for what seemed a lifetime. I was so excited, and my heart was pounding fast. Then, suddenly, there he was. Dressed in his flaming orange dress, he appeared to be so very small. As he came closer and closer, larger and larger, I thought I would swoon.

My eyes never left him. I took out my camera and started clicking away. I could see him through the lens; he was watching me, looking directly at me. He stopped abruptly in front of me and I froze. He reached over and took the little note from my hand. He looked directly into my eyes for a moment and then sat in his chair

'Sruti Ram as a young seeker.

at the head of the congregation. He gave some words of welcome and expressions of love, got up, and left to go inside to his rooms. I was so thrilled by this recognition. I automatically assumed that the rest of my time there would flow equally well.

Many people came over to me and assured me that Baba was treating me in a very special way. Well, folks, it was a setup. No matter what I did after that, I could not get Baba's attention. I think if I had appeared naked and danced a jig, he would not have given me a glance.

I purposefully plotted somehow to touch his feet. To touch the feet of the guru is one of the most important acts to accomplish as, traditionally, the guru dispenses the gift of intense energy in this manner. I studied his every move and knew what door he would come out of each day. I would sit right at the threshold, waiting to leap onto his feet. Of course, on that day he would not come that way. I would hide behind a large person waiting to ambush him on one of his walks. That day, he would not take a walk.

I tried to capture his attention for many weeks, but to no avail. I did, however, witness many miracles. Baba would manifest sacred ash from out of the air and administer it to the many devotees who cherished the magical substance. There would be miraculous healings of multitudinous diseases. He would manifest articles of gold and diamonds as talismans for many people. These miraculous events were so numerous that we would gather at the end of the day to compare notes. "How many miracles did you see today?" became an ordinary question.

The season changed, and Baba moved to his other ashram in the desert at Puttaparthi. I followed with the trail of Westerners.

One day I went to the *mandir*, prayer hall, for morning prayers. I was feeling really left out and my ego had been crushed by my failure to obtain another glance from the guru, much less ever hope to get a private meeting with him. To think that I had thrown it all away back in Bombay in order to go and have some fun in Goa. I was despondent over my weakness of purpose.

On the outside of the mandir was a huge statue of Ganesh, the elephant god who is the remover of obstacles. I stood there while I said my prayers and was overwhelmed with tears. I confessed my sorrow for being so unappreciative of the original plan for my deliverance to his abode. I had not fully recovered from my confession when the time was at hand to get a place in the hall so we could have darshan. I sat in the third row with the men and continued to wait for his arrival.

We started to chant. I was still spinning from the earlier communion with Ganesh, so I closed my eyes, tried to steady myself and sing along. A feeling of nausea and heat filled my body. I felt as though I would puke right there in the temple. Hotter and hotter, sitting with my eyes closed and swaying from side to side, I decided to get the heck out of there before I made a complete fool of myself. As I lifted my head and opened my eyes, I was amazed and shocked to see Sai Baba standing directly in front of me. I gazed into his eyes—the loveliest, sweetest eyes I could imagine. He smiled and gently lifted his garment to expose his feet. He said one word: "TAKE."

My mind reeled and I wept at the great gift. I touched his feet with my right hand and then touched my forehead with that hand. He smiled again. He turned away, sat on his chair, and calmly continued to do what he always did: smile. He loved everybody.

My body cooled down. I returned to my room and meditated for the rest of the day. A feeling of great love and completion permeated my being, and all was well with my world.

Several days went by in the normal ashramic way, and then word came that Baba was leaving and going back to Bangalore. As usual, I made arrangements to share a car with other people. We were three people and the driver. A doctor named David sat in the front with the driver, while an older woman with a very thick German accent shared the back seat with me.

About an hour into the trip across the desert, I started to have severe chest pains. I tried to deal with it, but it got worse and worse. Finally, I asked the driver to stop for a moment. Dr. Dave examined me. He listened and touched my chest here and there. By now I was in a heavy sweat.

"Well, George," he said, "I think you're having a heart attack."

I was quite frightened by this development. "Oh, great," I thought. "I'm going to die here in the middle of the desert. My poor mom will probably never even get to see the body. Woe is me."

Surprisingly, the nondescript German lady suddenly came to life and said, "You must be the one." With that, she took a small vial out of her bag and said, "Here, drink this. It's from Baba." Without hesitation, I took the little bottle and gulped it down. Within seconds I had relief. Then she told us the story about the magic elixir.

The night before we left the ashram she had been called to Baba's room. He told her to go to the car area and look for car No. 18, secure a seat in that car, and take the bottle of medicine with her. He said, "Give it to George when he has his heart attack. It's not a normal attack, but a karmic opening of his heart. This will ease the pain of the experience."

The level of knowing and love shown to me by my Baba blew me away. I was amazed and delighted. What a way to have a personal and direct experience of a miracle! I was also quite relieved to be spared the continuation of the heart attack. We continued on to Bangalore and all went well. I felt quite good for the next few days. The sense of being loved and nurtured permeated my body and mind. And I never did have a heart problem again.

Looking back and thinking about my very first darshan with Sathya Sai Baba, the fact remains that my insignificant note that he accepted was a very direct connection to the heart of the matter. My heart *was* truly open to him. I guess he noticed.

RamRam.

Miracles do happen. Be grateful when one does. Let yourself be flooded with gratitude: A miracle is proof of the divine unity of all beings.

CHAPTER 5

RELIVING THE PAST

I BECAME FRIENDLY with two other Westerners during my stay in Bangalore, and my new friend Hal and I decided to travel further south together to have some adventures. It was great fun. We got on a train, slept all night in our private compartment, and awakened in Madurai, a city famous for a very majestic temple dedicated to the goddess Meenakshi. The edifice is completely adorned with thousands of sculptures. I think it is the largest temple in India.

It was the time of *Shivaratri,* the Hindu festival of the god Shiva, one of the biggest celebrations in India. Everything was really charged with energy. People and animals alike were bedecked with ornaments and flowers. The elephants and cows were resplendent with color and jewels. We elected to attend the celebration at the temple, but we were told that only Hindus could enter the inner sanctum. Of course, that aroused my desire. I wanted to see and feel the inner sanctuary.

The temple itself was huge. In the center of the walled area was a beautiful pool, very large and ornate. There were steps on all sides, and pilgrims from all over India were bathing in the pool, as is the custom before attending a *puja* (ritual). Naturally, we complied with tradition. As we had been in India for some time, we really looked like Hindus; I was very dark-skinned after my experience at the beach in Goa. In order not to give myself away as a Westerner, I chose to be *mauna*, a discipline in which one remains silent.

After being properly washed and dressed, we entered the main hall. There before us was an enormous statue of the bull Nandi, Shiva's vehicle, at least twenty feet high. Pilgrims were circumambulating the image, so we joined in. It was very hypnotic. The throngs of people made it very difficult to see anything but the statue. While walking around it, I noticed a small archway in the stone wall that supported the statue. I signaled to my friend Hal and suggested that we see where it led. He was not very happy about the idea and I almost had to drag him to the doorway.

Upon entering that portal, we saw a stone stairway going down into the lower levels of the temple. The steps were covered with a thick layer of dust and it was evident that they had not been used in a very long time. Protesting all the way, Hal was pushed and prodded down to the bottom. He was petrified; I was fascinated and excited by the risk and the feeling of adventure.

The stairway took us to a long, dark, cathedral-like space. There were many smaller rooms all along the sides of the main hall—little temples, if you will, like those of a Christian cathedral. With the help of a searchlight, we stumbled through this great hall until we came to a huge painted gate, secured in the center with a chain. The gate was old and ornately painted with gold symbols. I managed to pry it a bit and squeeze through.

Hal was flipping out. "We should *not* be here. We are going to get into a lot of trouble. Let's get out." But he could not dissuade me from entering the space behind the barrier. I was filled with an uncontrollable desire to enter that place. Just inside the gate there was a chamber about twenty feet square. Many cushions in parallel lines were facing the front of the room, where a kind of swing with a single cushion on it was suspended from the ceiling by chains. It was obviously a place where the priests would sit in attendance to the person on the swing. It was clear that this room had not been used in many, many years. Dust and cobwebs covered everything like a blanket.

Poor Hal was beside himself and refused to go any further. I, on the other hand, could not monitor my irresistible urge to sit on that swing. I carefully mounted the floating platform and gingerly situated my butt on the cushion. The pillow immediately disintegrated to a flat pile of dust. Nevertheless, I sat there and closed my eyes.

Immediately I was transported to another time and space. I became a very old man and the room was filled with priests sitting in repose. The entire chamber was alive with chanting and the heavy scent of incense permeated the room. I am not quite sure how long we were there, but it was a glorious happening. Finally, I opened my eyes and Hal was standing back at the gate, more nervous than a frightened deer.

He kept calling to me. "George, come on out of there. Hurry up. This is not a good thing. Oh boy, if we are caught here, I can't even think of the consequences." Finally, I carefully got up, walked slowly back to the chained gate, and asked him, "Did you hear the chanting? Did you smell the incense?"

"Oh brother, you really are crazy. Come on, let's get out of here."

We scurried along back to the stairway and up to the main hall and the large statue of the bull. Fortunately, no one noticed us returning and we joined in the procession again. I was just flying. *What was all that about? Did I revisit a past life, or what?*

A few moments later we followed the crowd into an even larger hall where the *pujari* or priest had just finished a ritual. As usual, the congregation was waiting for the *prasad* (blessed edible offerings) given by the pujari to the people who were attending the ritual. There were many very well-dressed Indian businessmen waiting for their share. I was standing on the side, observing it all, still reeling from my past-life episode. Abruptly, the priest turned away from the others and walked over to me, extending his arms that were holding the large tray of prasad, wanting to give me some. All eyes were now on me. I was dumbfounded by the attention. Our eyes met and he spoke to me in Hindi. I had no idea what he was saying and could not answer, as I did not speak the language well enough. I wasn't even supposed to be there in the inner sanctum.

I decided to assume the feeling that I experienced in that lower chamber, that of the old man on the swing. With that attitude, I gestured to him that I was not speaking and then extended my right hand, open with the palm up. He nodded to me respectfully and placed some of the blessed food into my hand. He nodded again, looked me in the eye for a moment, and turned to proceed with the distribution of the prasad to the others.

It felt as though we had really met in that moment. I, too, turned and consciously walked toward the archway and out of the temple. At this point, Hal, although relieved, was on the verge of a nervous breakdown.

When we finally got a distance away from the temple, I came back to myself and realized what had just gone down. I knew in my heart that I had been in that place before, and I felt totally at peace with the course of events. After some time, I was able to comfort Hal and promised him I would behave in the future. All was well again with his world.

I, on the other hand, started to realize how absolutely comfortable I was in India. It embraced me and welcomed me. I was *home* again and was even more curious as to what would happen next.

We continued to travel around and eventually arrived in a place called Trivandrum. Hal was getting tired of traveling and wanted to stay put for a while, so we found a small house on the beach and thought we would rest there for a week or two. After a few days, the small village became very familiar and friendly.

It was getting really hot there. One day I wanted to take a walk on the beach, so I took a small bag of food and my camera and set out to have an all-day jaunt alone. It was so beautiful, and the ocean was so expansive. I walked for hours, resting here and there, meditating for a while and then continuing to walk. After many hours of exploration, I was exhausted and decided to nap on the beach. It was getting dark when I was awakened by a gentle nudge. I opened my eyes and standing before me was a native man wrapped in a small piece of cloth. Startled, I inquired as to where I was and who he was. He motioned to me to follow him. Nervously, I followed him to a small hut just down the beach. It was obvious that he lived there with his wife and three children, whereas I was a temporary resident on the beach.

There was a language barrier, but after some time we managed to communicate. He told me he was at the beach to collect coconuts and then return to his home in the jungle. I told him that I was a writer doing an article for a magazine and that I was expected back in a short while. I thought that the story about being a writer and that other people were aware of my absence would give me some protection. I was mildly fearful about being out there by myself. Shortly thereafter, several other men appeared in the hut. We all sat around together, and he told them about my "magazine project." They were all delighted to think that they would be in my article and insisted that I take pictures of them. I clicked away until I was out of film.

Suddenly a bottle of *feni* appeared. It was a local, potent, 95 percent-alcoholic drink made from coconuts. We proceeded to get quite drunk and ultimately fell asleep like a group of puppies in a stupor. All seemed right with the world.

The young seeker in the 1970s.

The next morning the men were ready to return to the jungle. Far off in the distance I could hear music. They said it was from their village and encouraged me to follow them home. We walked through the jungle for what was to become quite a long distance, crossing rivers and then walking more. It was very scary. All I could think of was my mom back home. If I disappeared, no one would ever find my body. What to do?

Eventually we arrived at a primitive village, consisting of several huts. In the center of the village was a fascinating concrete structure, about ten feet square, with a thatched roof. It had a knee-high wall around it with a wooden door on one side. I stood in front of it, not knowing what to do next. All eyes were on the stranger who had returned with the men.

I closed my eyes and centered my heart on the vibration that permeated the space. Amazingly, a great peace came over me. Again,

I focused my energy and suddenly I knew what to do. I approached the shelter and opened the door slowly. Much to my astonishment, enshrined within was a huge statue of Kali, the Divine Mother. Ferocious in appearance, she was adorned with garlands of flowers on top of the traditional skulls, arms, and legs that were carved into the statue.

Oh brother, I thought, *Kali worshipers*! I got past my mind and then again was guided by my spirit to the appropriate action. I reached into a large pot beside her that was filled with black ash. With hands cupped, I raised my hands over my head and then rubbed the ash all over my body until I was quite blackened. Then I fell to the ground, face down, with my hands folded in a prayer-like fashion, arms reaching out towards the image. I lay there for a moment and seemed to be transported to another time.

When I stood upright again, there was a resounding cheer from the gathering of folks. They all rushed to me and embraced me as though I was a long-lost child who had returned home. After a while, the women of the village appeared with large banana leaves laden with a variety of foods. All the food was placed before the idol, prayed over, and then dispensed amongst us. We consumed the feast offerings with great gusto. I was escorted to a hut and left alone to sleep till morning.

Upon awakening, I made it clear to the men that I had to return to those waiting for me back at the beach house. Two of them escorted me back through the jungle to the exact place where I had napped on the beach. They waited until I was out of sight and then started their long walk back. It was almost dark when I finally got back to my friendly and familiar house.

Hal was frantic and wanted to know all about my adventure. I told him everything and was really happy to hear it again myself. So much had happened, and I wanted to remember it all. As I told Hal the unbelievable course of events, I was awestruck by the magic of it all. To think that I had traveled into the depths of that jungle with a group of strangers to have this exceptional experience with the Divine Mother Kali! It was too fantastic. I was far away from everything familiar, in a strange culture, and yet so totally protected and cared for. It was getting very obvious to me that there was a power greater than anything I had ever known previously at work here.

After a couple of weeks spent traveling in South India, I was anxious to return to Baba. When I saw him again, it was so very wonderful. He was very kind to me, and I felt that finally I was ready to commit to a life in India at the feet of the Master, forever.

The day that I came to this decision was, of course, the day that it all changed again. In the *kirtan* hall, Baba stopped as he was passing me. He turned and said, "It's time for you to go home, back to America."

I almost fainted.

He continued, "Go home and worship your mother as though she were a goddess."

This was doubly shocking; I had never told him that one of the reasons I went to India was to get away from my mother. I did not want to leave him, but, being the obedient student, I soon returned home to the United States.

If you are called to enter a room, enter that room. You may not always know how or why, but accept it, as I did. Slowly, what happened to me began to mold my psyche, and I began to accept that I was forever going to be changed. Acceptance is one of the most important lessons a person can learn in a lifetime.

CHAPTER 6

ISN'T THAT EASY?

T HE REENTRY INTO Western culture was very difficult indeed. The spiritual path was so supported and recognized as an essential way of life in India. Living in my mother's home in New York was another trip altogether.

Mom was a very powerful and domineering type of person. Loving and kind, but a force to be reckoned with. She was an executive at work, quite accustomed to having her orders followed to the letter. Soon she recognized that I was not the same person I'd been before I left for India. And soon she began to object to my new-found foreign ways. She found the smell of the incense, the strange music and chanting and, of course, the building of a major altar in my bedroom a bit too much to bear. I'm sure she thought I had somehow become mentally disturbed and would need some kind of medical intervention. And in retrospect I do think that the replacement of my Jesus picture with that of a Hindu guru was the last straw. She was a devout believer in Jesus Christ. But she was making my life terrible, and I was probably having the same effect on her.

Hilda was my only refuge, an ocean of love and understanding. Her council would be golden to me—and I sought it. She and Mom had already established a good rapport, and I was certain she would know what I should do. "Hilda," I petitioned her, "my mother is just impossible. She hates the incense, music, and pictures. It's unbearable there. I just don't know what to do."

"Oh, dear," Hilda said. "This is an easy one. I'm so glad you came to me with this."

I felt instant relief. "I knew you would have the answer, Hilda," I said. "What should I do?"

"First of all, stop burning the incense. Take down the pictures. And stop playing that strange music. Oh yes, and chant quietly to yourself. There, isn't that easy?"

At first I was really shocked: Deny these amazing new parts of my life? I was a bit disappointed that my teacher would go against me that way. But of course, Hilda was quite correct. I was reminded of Baba's last orders to me: "Worship your mother." A good student doesn't question the teachers who have proven themselves to you, you just accept it. I found myself feeling deeply humbled by the wisdom of both of these teachers.

Sruti Ram with his mother, Rose.

So I returned home and slowly changed my behavior in Mom's house. The pictures came down, the incense disappeared, and the music was never heard again. The most beautiful change was not in the environment, but in my relationship with my mother. From that time on, we became best friends. I can honestly say that we grew closer day by day. I never regretted listening to the advice from my dear friend and teacher Hilda.

Baba Ram Dass was around the New York scene a lot in those days, and I became very close to him. He invited me to join him on some of his meditation tours and workshops as the meditation master for the retreats. It was a great time and led me into a very close affiliation with Neem Karoli Baba (Ram Dass's guru) and most of Baba's devotees in this country. Neem Karoli Baba, who we call Maharaji, is the focus of Ram Dass's bestselling book *Be Here Now*. Although I was usually in the company of Maharaji's satsang, I was still the Sai Baba guy. It did not really matter to anybody who my guru was; we were just one family.

I continued to attend Hilda's meetings and our relationship grew closer and more intense. On one occasion, I approached Hilda and confided that I wanted a deeper experience. I became her devout student. She taught me many practices and, consequently, I developed various yogic abilities, one of which was the ability to see into other people's minds, known as the activation of the third eye. I had been told stories about this, but now it was part of my life.

In my private times with Hilda, which were many, we would sit together in her room and she would relate stories of her experiences in India with various teachers. Hilda would sometimes reveal herself to me. Through my newly acquired third-eye power, I could see her in many forms. She was able to respond to many forms of her past lives and the wonders of her experiences from those times.

It was a very intense phase in my life that lasted for a few years.

But to be perfectly frank, these were extremely tricky times. The development of yogic powers involves intense breathing techniques, hours of meditation and study, and then, suddenly it seemed, the manifestation of incredible abilities. The shift, for me, was alarming—and confusing. Unexpectedly, I could read minds, control situations at will, and orchestrate events to my liking. Admittedly, it was fun at first. But then the ego came into play.

I can remember walking with Ram Dass in the city, on our way to a class. There was going to be a large gathering that morning, and we were carrying some large posters and pictures of gurus and teachers. The weather was threatening, and it felt like it was going to

Sruti Ram (seated, left), Ram Dass (standing), and Krishna Das (seated, right) at a Ram Dass retreat.

rain. But the rain would ruin our posters and pictures. We walked faster, and I thought to myself, *Well, I'll just stop the rain.* I uttered a mantra, and sure enough, the rain subsided.

"No, Sruti Ram," interrupted Ram Dass. "You can't do that! You cannot affect the natural order, the divine order, to suit your personal desires. It's against all the rules. It's detrimental to the natural scheme of things and it will be harmful to your development as a higher being."

I knew he was right, and I got it immediately. I said another mantra, and the rain returned. The posters and the pictures got wet as we continued on our way.

Ram Dass had served me a gigantic lesson. It was an illuminating moment for me that I would never forget. When we think that the power is ours, that we are the source and we can use it to serve our personal ideas of how things should be, we're making our own monster. History is filled with maniacal personalities who went astray with the abuse of power. I certainly did not want to join that fraternity.

These newly acquired abilities were not all fun and games on another level as well: they made life an assault on my senses. I would walk down a city street and hear the thoughts of hundreds of people simultaneously, and I could tell when someone was lying to me or working at cross purposes. It was terrible to know someone's ulterior motives like that. It was maddening.

Eventually I learned how to be far more disciplined in manipulating these gifts, and that discipline would serve me well as a teacher. In due course, an understanding developed—and the image of being Krishna's flute, and not just my own destructive ego, saved me.

Being the conduit for the dispensing of Divine energy with a humble attitude enabled me to proceed for years as a servant of the Divine. And in time, the practices that enabled these aspects

Sruti Ram in the early 1970s; "Have as much fun as you can" was his third guideline, after "Support the Dharma" and "Keep love in your heart."

to develop were abandoned—and I returned to a state of normalcy. I no longer required a mystical prowess to be who I wanted to be. My own development as a servant of God had become my focus. The best way to teach was to be. I have always felt blessed to have been involved in a spiritual community where the teachings of the masters were the main focus.

We are all one.

When we find the real deal, miracles occur fast. But the benefits remain with us forever.

CHAPTER 7

LEAVING THE ALTAR

I WAS DRIVEN for years. I was having a blast being one of the kings of the New York City mystical scene. Rock stars have groupies, gurus have devotees. I'd go to people's houses and see my photo on their altars, in their bedrooms. My picture was everywhere.

But I was thinking to myself, *watch out.* The program is self-realization, not success. My goal was not this kind of adoration at all. My head wasn't into sex and rock 'n' roll. Actually, I was celibate then, but I was lusting for self-realization, for spiritual development, not for bodies. But desire was all around me: *That one's a beauty. Isn't she a beauty? Isn't he a beauty?*

To fight the temptation I'd go right into a mantra. If you think about holy things, you're back in the safety zone—because darkness can't live in the light. And I was truly happy to be free of all of this. The more I saw of it, the more cautious I got. I realized that I was becoming a bit too powerful in the devotees' world.

Even on the path, some people just want someone to do the work for them. To give them *shakti*, to fill them with meditation and mantra. But it's your presence, your work, your sincere intention that's making it happen. It's not theirs. They're seeking, you're dispensing. It's great for them, not so great for you.

When I realized what was going on, that was it. It was 1978.

I shut the whole thing down and ran away. I wound up in Fort Lauderdale. One of my students, Allan, begged me to let him come down to Florida and join me, and I agreed. He drove my 1972 Firebird all the way down there, and I got him an apartment. We became partners and stayed together for twenty-one years.

It was a new life. I worked as a hairdresser in a top salon in Pompano Beach. And I called Ram Dass. I told him, "I walked away from the whole thing. I sent everybody home."

"Congratulations, Sruti Ram," he said. "You could have lived on that throne for the next three incarnations."

I would soon find my way back to my spiritual path, sure enough. But when I returned, it was on my own terms.

It's not that there's a little bit of Krishna in a spider and more in an elephant. Krishna lives in every living thing equally.

CHAPTER 8

THE SOUND OF TRUTH

WHEN I WAS given my second—and permanent—Hindu
name: *Sruti Ram*, I received it under the most profound and
moving circumstances. But even in our remarkable world, politics
can get in the way and loyalties are tested. For the sake of someone
I love dearly, part of this story must be left untold. But it was a revelation, and it did change my life, and that's what really matters. And
what the name means connected me even more closely to my path.

SRUTI: THE SOUND OF TRUTH

The word *sruti* is a Sanskrit word associated with Hindu sacred texts
and music. The srutis are considered the cosmic sounds of truth that
were passed on by the ancient *rishis* (the Hindu saints and sages).
They reside at the spiritual core of Hinduism and formed the basis
for the *Upanishads*—our ancient Hindu texts. All of the knowledge
contained within were revealed through direct experience—the srutis, these primordial and essentials truths, were heard. They are the
earliest teachings we know.

And in music, srutis are the sounds in between the notes. They
are the energy that holds a composition together.

RAM: THE SEVENTH INCARNATION OF LORD VISHNU

Ram became deified during the eleventh century but existed centuries before that. He manifested here on Earth to restore the dharma of humanity and destroy the evils present on earth so humanity could return to its primal activity: the realization of Divinity that resides within every human.

He is considered the embodiment of truth, morality, an all-around perfect ideal man and king.

To know without a doubt that you have been blessed and to realize your teacher and your connection to that Divine energy that we call GOD—what a great moment that is in a life!

CHAPTER 9

TO KNOW WITHOUT A DOUBT

I T WAS THE Hindu holiday of *Guru Purnima,* a day when all teachers are honored by singing sacred poems and songs together and then having a wonderful Indian feast. Many of us had gathered at a home of a friend and were enjoying the day. Shortly after dinner, I recommended that we all share a guru story. After all, it was the gurus' day and we did not all have the same guru. Why not tell some stories?

We sat in a circle around the large room. One by one, the tales flowed. It was so communal; we were really a family. My opportunity was at hand. There wasn't anyone there who did not expect to hear some fantastic miracle story about Sai Baba from my lips. I sat up straight and began to relate my tale. "As you all know, my guru is Neem Karoli Baba. Oh, what am I thinking? Sorry, folks, just a slip of the tongue."

I collected my thoughts and began again, "My guru is Neem Karoli Baba." Now I had everyone's attention. I wondered what was wrong with me. I started again. "Well, I am here to tell you that no matter how hard I try to say anything else, the only words I can say are: My guru is Neem Karoli Baba."

Without exaggeration, I must have tried fifteen times to say what all gathered expected to hear, but only Maharaji's name would come out. Finally, the true purpose of that experience exploded into my head and I got the message loud and clear:

MY GURU IS NEEM KAROLI BABA!

My body shook and I could not believe what had just occurred. Maharaji had just revealed one of the most important facts of my incarnation in a very direct and demonstrative fashion. I could think of nothing else and the words resounded over and over in my head. He is my *Satguru*—the one most important teacher for me above all others. He has chosen me.

At last, the miracle was truly evident. I was filled with awe and gratitude and a kind of *shanti* or peace.

My friends were amazed. No one was really sure what had happened, but I was sure. I could feel and taste it. I was in a state of euphoria. And I knew beyond the shadow of a doubt that he was my true Sat Guru.

Neem Karoli Baba.

A person can have many teachers in a lifetime, many gurus. But there is only one Sat Guru and I had just recognized mine. It was the start of a new life for me. Here we go, I thought, yet another new life. *Where will this lead me now?* But I was fearless. I had just had the thrill of a lifetime. Even today the excitement of that moment is fresh and alive—not just a memory, but a viable moment, ever new and powerful.

I got back to my home and, with no questioning at all, the pictures of Sai Baba were replaced on the central part of my altar, although I still viewed him with respect and reverence.

I knew that I had been chosen by Maharaji and was completely delighted. It was absolutely beyond all reasoning. No matter what my mind or anyone else's could explain, I knew it was real.

When something happens in truth, nothing can alter the fact in your heart and mind. The recognition and acknowledgement of one's Satguru is one of the most glorious moments in the life of a seeker. It is undeniable and self-evident.

CHAPTER 10

SHOPPING FOR HANUMAN

THERE IS A temple to Hanuman in Taos, New Mexico. Housed in the delightful building is one of the most beautiful *murtis* (statues) of Hanuman, the Hindu Monkey God, which I have ever seen. It is a place where my *gurubhais* (guru family members) congregate to celebrate the religious festivals that we have all taken as our own. It is a custom to dress the murti in new clothes for various occasions. Over the years, my friend Ganga Ram and I have delighted in securing the cloth from which Hanuman's clothes are made. In the Indian tradition, this is a great honor.

As usual, we set out to find the best and most beautiful silk available. We frequented a particular shop in Taos that was known to have many fine fabrics from all over the world. After perusing the goods for several hours, we found the perfect cloth—deep purple printed with a design in real gold. It was extremely expensive, but what the heck, it was for God.

Now that we had the cloth, we needed the trim to finish it off. I was told by the salesperson that all the trim was in a freestanding wardrobe. I opened the doors and, lo and behold, before me was an image of an Indian deity in the middle of the various trimmings. I stood there mesmerized. I couldn't understand what it was doing there. This shop did not sell statues and, if they did, why put it where no one could see it?

"Hey, Ganga Ram, come take a look at this." He was equally shocked and confused. I called across the shop, "Excuse me, miss, could you tell me something about this statue?"

"What statue?" She dutifully came over and was totally surprised by the image in the closet. "I have been here for years and I've never seen that statue before. Do you know who it is?"

"I sure do. It's Ramachandra, Lord Ram. Is it for sale? If it is, I would like to have it."

Holy mackerel, I thought. Here I am buying clothes for Hanuman and a statue of Ram appears before me. I really wanted that statue. I wasn't even sure why I had to have it, but I knew it was mine.

"I'll ask the owner of the shop and get back to you. It is really curious. I know I have never seen it before."

I was a little annoyed, but I had to wait. We left the shop with our purchases and returned to the temple. There is much to do for one of these *bhandaras* (festivals) and soon I was lost in the many preparations.

Eventually, the day of the bhandara was at hand. It was customary to bathe the statue of Hanuman before dressing it. The honor was given to Ganga Ram and me. Sitting on the sun porch while waiting for Ganga Ram so we could begin the ritual, I saw him walking towards me with a small package under his arm. "Here, Sruti Ram, this is for you."

It was the statue of Ram. My friends were quite taken with the beauty of it, and Jayant, a dear friend, exploded with delight. "How wonderful! Ram has come to the bhandara. This is very auspicious."

Then his wife saw the image and exclaimed, "Oh, yes, this image should live here at the temple. It is very important."

"Wait a minute," I said. "This statue is going to live with me in my home, and that is for sure." I knew that this was a very important happening in my life and I was firm about ownership. Ganga Ram and I then commenced the ritual bathing of Hanuman and, of course, the new image of Ram also was bathed and received the full ritual of that weekend. When the celebration was over and I returned home to the East Coast, Ram became a permanent member of my family.

At first, I had difficulty finding the right place for my new friend. He really demanded a special place. After much careful consideration, I gave him a home on a mantle. Little by little, he called to my attention. I started to think of him as a human family member. Odd, I know, but it was a private little game I played just between the two of us.

He looks cold. He needs some clothes, a coat or something. So, I acquired a sewing machine and started to fashion clothes for my friend. *Boy, this is pretty wacky*, I thought, but I had to do it anyway. Believe me, I did not know how to sew, but I quickly learned. After a while, he was the best-dressed statue in the neighborhood. My human friends thought it was peculiar, but they knew I never was exactly run-of-the-mill. This went on for about a year. Although it was odd behavior, it felt absolutely right. I had the feeling that I had done something like this before, in another life. It seemed hidden

Hanuman clothed for a festival in Taos.

way back in my memory and was slowly coming forward and being revealed to me.

Some months later I was back again in Taos. After an enjoyable visit to the temple, I stopped in a shop in Santa Fe and saw a beautiful wooden temple box. *Wow, this would be perfect for my Ram—a proper home for him.* It was an eighteenth-century antique and it was really expensive, almost a thousand dollars. It was so costly that I really couldn't afford it, so I settled for a less pricey box. After I arrived home, it seemed wrong not to have gotten him the best box, so I phoned Santa Fe and changed the order and got the right one. Finally, the big day arrived. I dressed Lord Ram in his new clothes and installed him in his new home with great fanfare and rituals that had been revealed to me slowly over the year in meditations and reveries.

With a great sense of accomplishment and ease, I spoke lovingly to my friend. "Well, Lord Ramachandra, you have a proper home now. No matter what happens to us, whether we live in a cave or in a tent, you will always have a beautiful house."

I felt that I had completed something very important. I felt secure in knowing that "God" had a beautiful and permanent place in my life and, more importantly, in my heart. I really think that is what the box signified to me.

It was a time when my finances were more than a little tenuous and such a large expenditure was way out in left field; however, it felt great to shop extravagantly for a home for him.

Three weeks later I was at work in my studio and saw the mail truck arrive. I walked out and got the mail, which included a very legal looking letter from my mortgage company. *Uh-oh, what's this?* I braced myself for the worst and opened the envelope. It was a notice that my mortgage had been PAID IN FULL. A close friend, who was aware of my financial distress, had decided that he could afford to do this for me and paid the whole thing off.

I was almost numb from the shock of the good news. Then the higher reality hit me. I had bought Ram a beautiful home in spite of the cost and my doubt about the expenditure. He, my beloved Lord, in turn bought me one in return. As bizarre as that might sound, there was a basis here: Having complete faith in my spiritual practice made it all seem perfectly logical.

A few months before, I had become interested in the Indian prac-

This statue of Ram was waiting in Taos for Sruti to find him.

tice of *thakurji seva*, which supports the concept of serving an image of the Lord as an integral part of your life. You accept the presence of the image as an actual living entity and develop an intimate relationship with that image, which could spawn a variety of phenomenal events such as the one I had just experienced.

My relationship with the statue of Ram—in truth, a very real living entity in my life—grew more and more intense. I spent countless hours meditating with him.

One day a man who had recently moved into the neighborhood came to my house to attend one of the weekly chanting sessions that had been ongoing in my home for some twenty years at that point. I recognized him from satsang gatherings in Taos. I had never taken the time

Sruti with Shyamdas.

to get to know him, but he was an old-time devotee of my guru and now here he was at my door. We became fast friends and, much to my surprise, I discovered that he was a practitioner of a form of worship that was almost identical to what had been revealed to me. He, too, had a *swarup* or image that he worshiped in the same way. However, he was well versed in the practice and had made it a life study in India for some thirty years. I was fascinated by his knowledge, which he shared with me. Shyamdas was a great teacher and we remained dear friends until his passing in 2013.

The worship became more and more elaborate. It consumed more of my life and eventually became the primary focus of my time. It was, and still is, a wonderful journey into the realm of *bhakti*, devotion. I must confess that it was somewhat comforting that such a devotional method did exist in actuality somewhere in the world; it made my behavior seem a little less outrageous.

One extremely interesting part of this method is that it is never-ending. There is no end to the lengths a devotee can go to accomplish a greater depth of devotion. The ornamentation for the image, the prayers and chants are limitless. And the best part is that I already knew most of it through some sort of past-life memory.

When a devotee carries out a task with the intention of giving all the effort and benefits thereof to the glory of the Divine, that task becomes one of spiritual service.

On a grand scale—it's called *seva* in Hindu—a service is for the good of all people, not just our small and commonplace application to our personal lives. It's another example of the benefit of really listening to our hearts.

THE BIG TURNAROUND

IRETURNED TO Taos for a visit with my friend Ganga Ram. Another aspect of the visit was to meet an Indian man named Gurudat who had been very close to my guru for most of his life. He was visiting from India and had come to the Taos ashram to see the Hanuman murti in the temple. Ganga Ram invited Gurudat to his home for lunch and I jumped at the opportunity to have some private time with him.

I decided to ask my new friend and teacher to come into my room and observe my seva (service). Being well versed in spiritual practice and scriptures, Gurudat's opinion and advice would be extremely valuable to me. He entered the room and went directly over to the altar where Ram had been installed. He stood quietly, scrutinizing everything: how the altar was set up, the placement of ritual articles, and the ornamentation. The attention to detail was a crucial aspect of this type of practice. I was sitting quietly on the floor watching his every move. He looked at me and asked, "Where does he sleep?"

I showed Gurudat the accommodation for the image to rest in comfort.

"Excellent," he said. He became very still, as though in a meditative state for a few moments, then bowed and touched his head to the altar platform. "Do you have any questions, Sruti Ram?"

"Thank you, Gurudat. Yes, I do have a problem that I am anxious to discuss with you. I have always felt confident in this practice and enjoy it very much. It has come very naturally to me. I believe that I remember more than I am taught about it. And now with your approval, my question is even more important."

"Well, what is it?"

"Lately I have been concerned about my ego in all of this. Sometimes I feel proud of my accomplishment and that element of pride is troublesome to me. Can you help me with this, please?"

His eyes grew large and he became very concentrated. "You should be proud of your devotion and intensity of purpose. You are his devotee and he is pleased with you. That is what you feel. However, take your pride and visualize it as a precious gem. Put that gem in the treasure box of your mind and keep it safe from others. Show it to no one else. You can safeguard this by never doing this whole practice with other people present. Worship in private when you do the seva."

Wow! What an exquisite teaching! He managed to take pride, one of the sins of man, and turned it around to become a useful tool. To reverse the thought of something being negative and transform it to a positive aspect was so very helpful, understanding, and wise. It brought home to me that spiritual ego had an important place on the path: it could support a seeker and help to advance the practice.

It was also very clear how important it was not to judge situations that appear to be negative and to find the positive aspect held within that situation. This was an invaluable teaching that greatly helped me deal with my own ego as well as other aspects of life, both in the spiritual realms and the mundane.

The essence of the student's experience is far greater, far larger, and far more profound than the accomplishment of his ego's satisfaction and gratification.

CHAPTER 12

RAM SPEAKS

ONE DAY, AS I was sitting with "God," observing Ram as beautiful and well cared for, I suddenly saw something that I had never noticed before: He looked sad and lonely. I was acutely aware of his call for his partner, Sita. I could hear in my heart his command: *Please bring me Sita. I am missing the presence of pure nature in her purest form.* That is how I perceived it.

Where would I find a Sita for Ram here in the States? So, the search began. I called every shop that I could imagine would have such a statue and searched the Internet around the world, but I could not find the mate to my Ram.

Sita is the consort of Ram, as described in volumes of scriptures, especially as written in the Ramayana, an ancient epic tale about Lord Ramachandra and his exploits in India. The reading of his story is said to bring liberation to the soul. The Ramayana is also said to contain all the answers necessary to live a *dharmic* life today. In the Ramayana, Ram represents pure consciousness; Sita represents pure nature.

As the story goes, Ram and Sita are separated when the demon king Ravana kidnaps Sita and flies off with her to his kingdom of Lanka. Ravana represents the ego and the power of the uncontrolled senses of the human psyche. So pure nature has been taken by the ego and must be rescued by pure consciousness. A large portion of the story is about Ram searching for Sita, enlisting aid from many fascinating characters. Sita is finally sighted in the gardens of Lanka by Hanuman, who has leapt across the ocean after invoking the name of Ram. He quickly informs Ram of her whereabouts and a terrific battle ensues before Ram and Sita are reunited.

It came to me in a flash. I, like Hanuman, must cross the ocean to find Sita for Ram. In the story, Hanuman is the personification of pure devotion. So, it's no surprise that Ram, pure consciousness, enlists the aid of Hanuman, pure devotion, to rescue Sita, pure nature.

I had no desire to return to India and hadn't entertained the thought for years. Going to India was wonderful, but it wasn't a vacation. It was always an arduous journey. However, my mind was suddenly filled with a passionate desire to return and it seemed, at the time, that my motive was noble and extremely important. Of course, I was well aware that there was a lot more to it than the surface reason for the trip. The underlying purpose wasn't perfectly clear yet, but my level of faith and trust in the philosophy of devotion was evident.

The journey turned out to be very important in my development and in the discovery of many aspects of myself. I was being called back to India and I had to go. There was also a woman saint in India that I had wanted to meet for years. I was not growing any younger, and neither was she.

As usual, finances were a major consideration. Such a journey was expensive, both in time and money. It wasn't at all clear how I could pull it off, but I had faith that Ram would take care of it all. I mean it, I was *absolutely sure* that it would happen.

I had established a tradition within the structure of my satsang—a celebration that I held in my home every New Year's Day with chanting for eleven hours straight, followed by an Indian feast. About a hundred people usually attended. The energy built to a wonderful crescendo and concluded with a glorious experience of fulfillment and joy. Everyone present was blissed out.

It was January second, the day after the bhandara in my home. The celebration had gone very beautifully, and I was sitting in front of the altar having a chat with my guru, represented by a beautiful sculpture. Although my guru had left his body more than twenty-five years previously, He was still very much alive in my heart and life. "Well, Maharaji, I keep getting the message to go to India and find Sita for Lord Ram. I don't know how I'll get there, but if you want it to happen, I know you will make it manifest. It's up to you."

I was confident in his power and ability to make it happen.

I picked up a friend on our way to meet others for brunch. My friend noticed that I looked very pensive. "What's up, Sruti Ram? You seem lost in thought."

I explained my financial dilemma to her and how I felt compelled to go to India. She listened and then boldly stated, "I too think that it is very important for you to go. How much would it cost?"

I picked a number out of the air. "About four thousand dollars."

"That's no problem for me," she said, and proceeded to write a check for the full amount. "Have a great trip," she said as she handed it to me, and we went off to brunch.

I sat in the restaurant, amazed at how fast my guru and Lord Ram had manifested my passage to India. It wasn't a surprise that it happened, but it was unbelievably swift and left me spinning with delight. I called one of my teachers in India and told him when I would arrive. He said all would be taken care of for me. Once again, I was flying on God's energy to India on a divine mission.

Needless to say, my attachment to the statue of Ram was a major consideration in planning my trip. I knew he had to join me on the pilgrimage. I secured a proper traveling box for him and packed all his accoutrements and a few things for myself and off we went.

I should have known that the trip would be blessed. Consider the episode at the airport security station. When Ram's box was scanned, the security person had to see what the heck I had in there. I carefully opened the box and showed Ram to her.

"Oh, that is really beautiful" she stated in a delighted tone of voice. "May I touch it?"

I really did not want him touched, but I said sure. She reached in and, ironically, touched his feet. *Wow*, I thought, *that's perfect*. She was immediately filled with an obviously pleasant energy and became very friendly and cordial. It really made me smile when, as we walked away from the security station, she said rather loudly, "I hope the both of you have a great trip."

I arrived in India safe and sound and was greeted at the airport by my driver and car, which had been arranged prior to my departure. There I was, back in India. What a gas!

The ashram was beautiful, and I was greeted warmly and well taken care of by the staff. It took only a few days before I was back in the swing of things and really happy to be back.

I was confident that I would have no difficulty finding a statue to match and mate my guy. Surprise, surprise. I was in Vrindavan, Krishna land, and there were no Ram statues around, much less one of Sita. This kind of search is no easy task; it's a constant journey in bumpy rickshaws on badly broken streets, while stuck in traffic jams with cows, goats, pigs, and cars. Radha and Krishna were everywhere, but no Ram and Sita. I searched high and low and figured that I would have to leave Vrindavan to look in another city.

Finally, I found myself in a jewelry store where they sold silver ritual items such as bells, trays, and incense holders, but no statues.

While I was paying for some items, the salesman and I chatted. "What made you come to India?" he asked.

"I came to see a great saint here in Vrindavan and to find an image of Sita for my Ram, my thakurji."

He was familiar with that word and was more than slightly surprised that this foreigner was a practitioner of such a formal method of devotion.

From the back of the shop a loud voice bellowed out a question. "What size did you want?"

"Eight inches tall."

"Just one moment, I have something to show you."

I was amused and curious but waited patiently while I continued to chat with the gent who was processing my purchases. There was a lot of banging of articles and rumbling around in the back room. It sounded like someone was wrestling back there. After about fifteen minutes, a small old man with a twisted face, quite hunched over, emerged from the back of the shop and announced, "Here is your Sita."

He placed the statue down in front of me. She was silver, exactly the correct size, and crafted in the style to be a perfect match for my Ram.

"How do I know that she is Sita and not Radha?"

He turned the statue around to show me the back. "Only Sita wears her *sari* in this fashion. She *is* Sita!"

I stared at the statue. "What part of India is it from?"

"I'm not really sure, but she has been here for seven years. She is the only statue in the shop. I think she has been waiting for you and her Ram to find her."

I studied the statue very carefully and searched my feelings about it. A feeling of great warmth filled my being and an enormous smile spread across my face. "Yes, I know now that this is the Sita I have been looking for. I'll take her home with me now."

The old man stood up as straight as he could and bellowed across the shop. "He came to India to find Sita, and he found her here!"

Hearing that statement, the people in the shop shouted joyously, *"Jai, jai Bhagavan!"* (Hail to the Lord!) Everyone was thrilled for me and considered this discovery a very auspicious event even for them, as they were all part of it. It was as though we had decided to have a party, and everybody wanted to participate.

What a stunning event and what an amazing culture! Everyone in the shop was genuinely thrilled and supportive. I was one happy guy and quickly outfitted the consort of my beloved Ram with all the proper clothes and jewels that the many deity shops in town had to offer. Can you imagine the delight in shopping for God? There are actually tailors for the statues. What a serendipitous aspect of Indian society. Anywhere else in the world, this kind of activity would be subject to incredible scrutiny and possibly disparagement.

I brought Sita home to the ashram, bathed her with rosewater, chanted mantras with unwavering devotion to the energy she represented, and immediately installed her on the altar in my room with her beloved Ram.

The fact that she had been in that shop for so many years without a mate was extremely unusual; these statues are always made in sets and sold in pairs. And the fact that they were both created in the same style flavored the episode with a delightful air of mystical power and coincidence. I was thrilled beyond belief. They occupied a very special place in my ashram room and consciousness.

The entire drama was saturated with what I like to refer to as mutual reception of energies, the harmonious merging of intention and manifestation. I could not help but observe the parallel of this situation with the search for Sita in the Ramayana. Sita had been rescued and reunited with her beloved Ram, just like in the scriptures. History had repeated itself in my consciousness and life.

I lay in bed that night playing back the entire movie. How wonderfully bizarre the entire drama was!

Soon word spread around the ashram that Sruti Ram had found the mate for his thakurji. Slowly but surely, all the elders came to my room to see her/them. They came to have darshan, a viewing of the sacred forms. It was well known that this was my reverent practice. One of the sweetest visits was from one of the elder mothers. She entered my room and sat down very close to the altar. She observed everything; then, after some time, she smiled, bowed her head reverently, and said, "Don't worry. Her looks will improve. She has been without him for a long time. She will get prettier in time."

How lovely! How utterly innocent and simple! This lady's simplicity was matched only by her devotion and elegance. It came to light later on that she was a well-educated *maharani*, a princess, which more than pleased me. There was no mistaking her for a simple-minded elderly person. And, by the way, she was correct about Sita's appearance. When Sita first arrived, she seemed to be frowning. I can tell you that, in all honesty, she did get prettier and now has a beautiful smile that is commented on by most people.

My practice leaped forward by many levels. The daily practice and the personal experiences that followed became yet more profound and insightful. I could feel the changes in my being and my body. I felt as though I could fly, and actually did in my dream state. But that's another story.

The limits of devout ritual are infinite and demanding. And the more I do, the more I want to do. But that is when the Divine speaks. You may experience it as a mind-altering jolt of magic, or it may feel like falling in love. Do not feel uncomfortable about establishing an actual relationship with a divine image. There may be miraculous consequences.

CHAPTER 13

THE HAND OF GOD

I N FEBRUARY 2003 I was in Rishikesh. It was an opportunity for me to see Siddhi Ma and to escape the cold wet weather of Vrindavan. On a beautiful sunny afternoon, I was about to go to the ashram to sing in the Hanuman *mandir,* as I had done every day for a month. Siddhi Ma had instructed me to come for prasad and to sing in the mandir every day. On this particular day, I asked a friend if I could use her car. It's quite a challenge to drive in India and I had never had the courage to do it before this visit. However, I had become quite used to driving there and actually enjoyed it immensely.

My friend had recently gotten a new car and really did not want anyone to drive it yet. She suggested that I use the motor scooter instead. It was a hybrid model, pretty quick on the pickup. Driving along in not very much traffic, I suddenly realized there was a car driving on the wrong side of the road heading straight towards me. I moved over to the right and so did the other car. I moved again and so did the car. Finally, just before a head-on collision, I ran off the road onto some gravel and lost control of the bike.

Sri Siddhi Ma, the incarnation of the goddess Durga and a living saint, was one of Sruti Ram's teachers, his friend, and his inspiration.

I sped into a chai (tea) shop—in one side and out the other. It was almost funny. Chairs went flying in the air and people were diving out of my way, kind of like a Three Stooges movie from my childhood. Finally, I stopped, with the bike on top of me, and regained consciousness; I guess I was out for a minute or two. The first thing I remember is seeing a *Shiva Lingam*—a sacred stone that is present in almost every temple in India. I looked a little to the left and saw an image of Ram. I thought, *I must be dead and fortunately I've gone to the right place.*

After a moment, a small thin Indian man lifted the bike off and helped me to my feet. He owned the chai shop and was very kind and helpful as he ushered me into the shop and sat me down. "What can I do for you?" he asked.

I was so dazed, the only thing I could think of was to have some chai. He quickly handed me some wonderful hot tea. He then insisted that he check my body for broken parts. I stated confidently that I was okay, but he persisted. He rolled up my pants and discovered that my legs were pretty badly bruised. My arms were in even worse shape. My elbow was completely torn open and bloody. He wanted to take me to the hospital, but I objected vehemently. Going to the hospital in India can be a very questionable undertaking. He cleaned and washed my wounds with a large bar of camphor. The wounds miraculously closed, and I felt no pain. Of course, later on it was determined that I was in shock.

After some time, I was able to get back on the bike and return home. I was tenderly cared for and rested for a few hours until it was time for us to go sing at the ashram. My friends and musicians counseled me not to go, but I insisted on going, although I felt pretty banged up. We arrived at the mandir and prepared to start the kirtan. Soon we realized that I could not perform my part very well.

I decided to go upstairs to look for Siddhi Ma. Although it was not yet time for her darshan, I found her sitting in the hall by her-self. She took one look at me and with great concern asked, "What happened to you?"

I recited the tale. She immediately sent me to the kitchen with the instruction: "Tell them to give you special chai." I obeyed and returned to her.

"How do you feel now?"

"I think I'm better."

"Go back to the kitchen and tell them you need special prasad."

Again, I did as I was ordered. Upon my return, she again inquired, "How do you feel now?"

"Really much better, Ma."

She instructed me to sit in the corner of the room and be still. I sat for about half an hour until she reappeared from the other room and asked over and over, "How are you now? Are you better now? Are you sure you feel better now?"

After many *yes, yes, yes* replies, she got very quiet and suddenly seemed to grow to an enormous size in front of me. She bellowed, "You are never allowed to drive in India again. Never! Only a taxi or chauffeured car is acceptable. Do you understand?"

"Yes, Ma."

"Are you sure?"

"Yes, Ma."

"Maharaji saved your life because you were coming here to sing the praises of Hanuman. You are very lucky. Never, never drive in India again."

I was shaken by the image before me. I could feel the power that emanated from her being. Then she got still. Suddenly, she pointed to the door and shouted in a very strong voice, "*Jao!*" That's a very strong order to "Go!"

I left the room marveling at the love and kindness that had been showered on me. She had taken care of me—she fed me, gave me rest, scolded me, and then sent me back home. The similarity of her persona with what I had learned about Maharaji dazzled me. I felt totally loved, cared for, and protected. When I finally did get home, I was astonished to see the condition of the bike and helmet. All the equipment was smashed up. Later I was diagnosed as having had a mild concussion.

A few weeks later I was in Rajasthan, sightseeing with friends. We had reached a place where the car couldn't go any further. Some of the boys had motorcycles and insisted that I ride with them up the mountain. I almost got on the bike, but then remembered my teacher's orders: "Only taxi or chauffeured car will do." I declined the ride and walked instead. Soon after, the boy who had insisted that I ride with him on the motorcycle had an accident and was injured.

Before I left Rishikesh I wanted to thank the wonderful *chai walla* who had treated me so kindly. I recalled his name was Shiv Ajit—Shiva the unconquerable. On the day of the accident I had offered him money, but he had refused to take it. This time I returned with an Indian specialty—a box of milk sweets—which he accepted in front of all with great delight. They were the kind of sweets I would bring to a guru or saint or Maharaji.

It was really clear to me that I had been protected and lovingly cared for by the Hand of God, which I feel is a constant in my life. Since I was fortunate enough to have a guru who gave me specific instructions, I learned never to disobey. It was a major lesson, a matter of faith and trust.

Giving credence to the mystical manifests benefits in the physical realm. When we obey our instincts and our teachers, the Divine steps in, freeing us from the burden of doubt.

CHAPTER 14

LESSONS IN GRACE

(or, Never Worry About Money)

IN EARLY 2004, as my life was moving along just fine, a phone call upended it once again. My dear teacher, Ram Dass, had recently suffered a stroke and needed to improve his living situation, so the plan was to move him from California to Maui. But he needed someone he could trust to help him there, and make sure the household was safe, comfortable, and well-maintained. Could I help make these arrangements?

I wasn't too keen on uprooting myself from my good life in the Catskills and relocating on an island in the Pacific Ocean. But after much deliberation and discussion I decided I had to go. I wasn't sure for how long, but I was committed to making sure Ram Dass was well-cared for.

The house we settled Ram Dass in was large and extraordinarily beautiful. It sat on the edge of the ocean in Haiku, a community on Maui, with fabulous views and lush plantings. It was all on one level and could easily accommodate Ram Dass and his wheelchair, with a great room in the center, and rooms extending on either side. And it felt private, but easily accessible.

Granted, Maui is unarguably beautiful, but running the house was a complex undertaking. Ram Dass was famous, brilliant and revered by so many people, but he also needed a lot of help. It was my job to arrange all the doctors and therapists as well as the cooks, groundskeepers, general maintenance people, and bookkeeping. I also booked appointments for the many people who requested private time with the baba, and planned, organized, and monitored the many events and special occasions that were held at his home.

Everything was kept in a daily appointment book, and it was usually packed. To get a break, I had to make sure there was someone to take my place for an hour or so, and then I could book time for myself. I'd drive to the ocean and just chill for an hour. Then it was back to my tasks.

I was always looking for ways to improve Ram Dass's care, and I suspected he wasn't getting enough physical exercise. After several discussions with his physical therapist, we decided to beef up his activity level, and I found a swimming pool to bring him to. It was ideal: The pool had a lift for getting in and out, though anyone who used it had to have their own special seat to fit it. I bought one, and explained the whole setup to Ram Dass. It's a great development, I noted, but he disagreed. He was not happy about going into a new and challenging situation. Though I explained how the lift worked, he was still concerned he would not be able to get out of the pool. His conclusion: He was not going to participate. But I countered that I'd already bought the chair, and I couldn't return it. "We're going," I said to my old, stubborn, and fragile friend, and he begrudgingly acquiesced.

Of course, before we got there, he repeated how displeased he was that I'd pushed him into this situation. But I insisted. Once in the water, he said, *"Well, what the heck do we do now?"*

"Lean on me, and let's walk," I said.

He put his arm around my shoulders and leaned heavily on me and we proceeded to walk the entire distance. It was a long way, and we took it slowly. He'd had great difficulty walking before this. Now he looked at me with the wonder of a child experiencing a first-time joy.

"Oh my God, Sruti Ram, I'm walking."

We made it to the far end.

"Now what?" he said.

"We go back to where we started," I said, and we did.

This was a remarkable shift for him. He had *moved his body*. Soon he was back up on the lift and out of the pool. The ride home was ecstatic—we were both thrilled with "our" accomplishment.

Soon, we were going to the pool twice a week, and thus began his recovery—which eventually led to his going to the beach to enjoy the sun and the surf. Those adventures on the beach, where Ram Dass was accompanied by a gathering of many people, were a glorious time for him. And they became a magnet for many people who wanted to be in his presence. Long after I had returned to the mainland, he was still going, and many would come to see him there.

My time with Ram Dass in Maui was filled with people arriving and leaving in a constant flow: famous personalities, devoted followers, curious seekers, old friends—an incredible mix of humanity. And, of course, there was always some new issue with running the household. I kept everything going, dealing with all the mundane problems while keeping his health issues front and center. There was always something demanding my attention, and that included how to fund his care.

A group of supporters worked constantly to raise money for the enormous expenses of running the household and holding events for Ram Dass. But one day, I realized we had a new problem. The balance in the checking account was low—and not enough to pay the rent. And the rent was coming due.

I had to tell Ram Dass. He was sitting in his bedroom, reading a book. I decided to just come out and say it.

"Baba," I began, "the rent is due, and we don't have enough in the bank to cover it."

He looked up from his book. "Uh huh," he said. Then he returned to his reading.

"Baba, I am not sure how to handle this," I said. "It's serious."

"Yes, I understand," he said, and then went back to reading.

Sruti Ram with Ram Dass at a festival in New Mexico.

I was getting more frustrated by the minute. "Look, baba, it's just the two of us here. There's no one else listening. So, you can be honest with me. What are we going to do?"

Ram Dass put the book down and looked at me with that strong, centered gaze I had come to realize was a sign he was about to make a powerful statement. "I never concern myself with money. Maharaji told me never to worry about money. Maharaji stated, 'All the money of the universe is available to you. Never worry about money.' So, I don't. And besides, I have you. *You* worry about it."

Then, again, he went back to reading his book.

Of course, this was not the answer I'd hoped for. I had no idea what I was going to do. Exasperated and out of options, I went back to my office in the house and sat at my desk. Above, on the wall, was a huge picture of Maharaji. I looked up at it and said out loud, "Well, we need your help. The time is now."

Still anxious, I decided to calm my brain by meditating. About fifteen minutes later, I suddenly had an idea. What about Social Security?

Social Security? I asked myself. Why on earth am I thinking about that?

I realized, though, that I hadn't seen anything in the account books about Social Security, and Ram Dass should have been receiving it. I hadn't seen any activity since I started doing the books. So, I got on the phone to start an inquiry. I explained the situation to the associate on the other end—about Ram Dass having a stroke and moving from the mainland, and all the confusion that had ensued as he changed his life.

"Is it possible any checks have been issued?" I asked the lovely woman on the phone.

"Well, yes," she said. "But they were all returned, unopened."

As I was talking, I could imagine Ram Dass in his bedroom, just calmly reading as this little maelstrom took place. But I also realized that no one had put in a change of address for him during his big move, and the fact had been overlooked for many, many months.

"Are these checks still available?"

"Yes," the woman at Social Security said.

"Could they be sent to the bank as soon as possible?"

"That would be very easy to do," she said. "I'll get to it right now."

Inside, I was very excited, wondering how much it could be. Outwardly, I kept my composure and stayed passive. "Would you mind telling me what amount will be deposited, just so I can look for it?"

The sum was enormous. It was several thousand dollars, she informed me.

"Thank you so much," I managed, before hanging up and nearly falling out of my chair. I floated into Ram Dass's room to tell him the wonderful news.

"Guess what I was able to do?" I asked him, beaming.

Slowly, he looked up from his book. And I caught that look again.

"And what did *you* do?" he asked.

I told him the whole story. At that moment, I was actually exposing a great deal of egocentric energy, because I was very proud of my own success. And part of me knew it, and I felt guilty already.

Ram Dass looked up from his book once again. This time, he stared directly into my being. "See?" he said, but with incredible love. And then, as before, he returned to his reading.

I left the room with tears of joy in my eyes. I realized something so profound and moving: Ram Dass never doubted Maharaji and his directions. His faith was undeniable, his trust was worthy and steadfast. Maharaji had said not to worry about money, and so he did not. And money came to him. This was grace.

This was a great lesson for me: When in doubt, rely on the power of faith and personal conviction. Let go of the ego and get out of the way. Let the grace, which we are all guaranteed at birth, energize and do the work it was meant to do. Grace is always there for us to tap into. Activate this energy by allowing the true self, the divinity within each of us to just be.

I must admit, Maharaji has never disappointed me either. Having access to a master like Maharaji is the blessing of a life-time—indeed, of lifetimes. And I am forever grateful.

CHAPTER 15

THE POWER OF THE NAME

O NE DAY, I was sitting around the ashram in Vrindavan with Jivan Baba, one of the old Indian devotees who had been with Maharaji for many years, when he decided to take us to a nearby temple for darshan of the deity there.

Jivan Baba was a particularly sweet longtime devotee of Maharaji. He was so very respected that everyone wanted to hang with him, if he was in the mood, of course.

He was one of the old-timers we could approach almost anytime and question about anything to do with ritual, custom, and where to shop for the best price. We all loved him so much. He always encouraged us to go to the sacred places and experience the joy of a holy journey.

There were a few of us, and we piled into several rickshaws. I had the pleasure of riding with Jivan Baba in a rickshaw built for two.

We rode along the streets and corridors of Vrindavan 's Loi Bazar, where the congestion of people, cars, animals, and rickshaws was unusually thick. Bouncing along in this primitive vehicle on this beautiful sunny day, we were chatting about ashram life in general when I suddenly had an uncontrollable urge to begin chanting the name of Ram. It really was a rather odd time to break out into chanting mode, but it felt right and Jivan Baba was quite fine with it. Actually, I was always "in mantra" internally, and it just jumped out into the physical realm for no apparent reason. I really think he enjoyed the spontaneity of this type of spiritual distraction.

We came to a very busy intersection. Now you must realize that a busy intersection in a bazaar is total chaos and a complete breakdown of order and courtesy. While we were trying to navigate the disorder and still have a pleasurable time of it, a man on a motorcycle came out of nowhere, traveling at breakneck speed and heading directly towards us. These random cyclists are the terror of the bazaars. Usually they are very young and defying the rules. The motorcyclist slammed on his brakes, and our two vehicles— his bike and our rickshaw—jolted to a stop, just gently kissing each other's fenders. This all happened in a split second.

Jivan, as startled as I was, looked at me and smiled. Our eyes met—and we knew that we had just been saved from very serious injury. It was evident to both of us that we had been spared a calamity. The motorcyclist was also surprised by our calm attitude, which influenced his response as well. We all smiled at each other and proceeded on our way. Let me just declare that this friendly exchange is not usually what would occur. We parted in great amicable energy and I continued to chant the holy name until we arrived safely at the temple.

I really liked the idea of having built-in radar and automatic protection—one of the many benefits to chanting the name or, as is said in India, *Hari Nam*, the name of God.

When we are in the Zone, infinite correlation takes care of us.

CHAPTER 16

ANOTHER THAKURJI

A FEW DAYS after the near crash of rickshaws in the bazaar, some new people arrived at the ashram. I had been in Vrindavan for a couple of months and realized that I still had not seen many of the sacred places in that area.

Vrindavan is the land of Lord Krishna and is called Braj. I really loved taking the new folks around and helping them get acclimated and accustomed to the new experiences of India.

I gathered up a bunch of Westerners and arranged for a car and a guide to take us on a *yatra*, a pilgrimage to sacred places.

After touring about all day, the guide finally got us to Govardhan, which I had been constantly asking to visit. There is a small mountain there, the hill that Krishna lifted and held above the monsoon-like rains that threatened to destroy that place and its people. The rain was caused by the god Indra and his anger with Krishna.

The hill still exists and is considered very sacred. As a matter of fact, many people have a stone from this hill in their homes and worship the stone as a deity. I had in mind to get a stone to keep in my temple, not so much to worship but rather so I could have that sacred vibration in my home.

We arrived at Govardhan Hill, in the town of Jatipura. The customary procedure is to walk around the hill itself, a distance of about six miles. It was late in the day, so we proceeded to the hill and found a narrow path on and around the rock formations there. I walked about in search of a stone. I was very particular about which one I would take home with me. I had seen rather large ones in people's homes and personally wanted a small one, as I was planning on taking it back to the US.

Finally, I came upon *the* stone. I had never seen anything like it. It was red in color, like the hill itself, and had eyes. Yes, *eyes*—the kind one can see on a ceramic idol in a temple—hand-painted eyes made of gold. This stone also was decorated with various symbols and had colors painted on it. Stunned by the appearance of such a beautiful offering, I took a piece of clean silk from my pocket, wrapped up the stone and put it out of sight. I did not share my find with the others. It was too wonderful, and I just wanted to be alone with it for a while before I shared the joy of finding such a fabulous stone. We continued exploring the hill, and then after about an hour returned to the ashram.

Upon returning, I saw Gurudat taking tea outside his room. I stopped to chat with him. He questioned me about where I had gone that day, so I told him all about our adventures and then showed him the stone that I had found.

He took it in his hand and perused it intensely, to my surprise. A bit wide-eyed, he proceeded to ask me, "Where did you get this stone? Did you buy it somewhere?"

"No, baba, I found it on Govardhan Hill."

"Just as it is? Exactly like this?"

"Yes, baba, just as you are seeing it now."

"This is a wonderful thing that has happened to you. He [Krishna] has manifested it for you. He must be very happy with you. However, you should know that you must perform special puja [ritual] for this stone and take very good care of it. I shall mention it to Sri Ma."

Sri Siddhi Ma.

I was amazed at the importance that my dear teacher put on the stone. I agreed that it was very attractive and unusual but had not realized the extreme importance of this sacred manifestation.

The next day I went to see Sri Siddhi Ma. She asked for all the details of my finding the stone and wanted to see it. I gladly showed it to her. She studied the stone and then she told me that it was very important—and that it should never leave Braj, India! If I took the stone back to America with me, it would create havoc in my life because it would be so unhappy. She, too, said it required special treatment to keep it properly. She asked, "What will you do with it?"

Realizing the seriousness of her demeanor I thought quite seriously and said, "I want to make sure that it gets into the right hands. To my mind, Ma, it should be with you. Please take it now."

She smiled and told me to keep it and do the puja that I do for Ram to the stone. She informed me that the sacred stone had come to me for a reason, most likely a very special blessing. She would take it when she was ready to leave the ashram in a few days.

When the time of her departure arrived, Ma sent her assistant to my room to tell me to bring the stone to her. I promptly obeyed and arrived at her door at the appointed time. I was ushered into her meditation room and sat at her altar. The sanctity of her personal temple was highly concentrated. It felt thick with energy, like walking into a room filled with Jello. I was instructed to place the stone there, and I was invited to meditate for a while. Siddhi Ma's puja was exquisitely simple. Much to my surprise, I could see that Ma did puja, ritual, to rocks. There were five or six fair-size stones there, placed very carefully around Maharaji's blanket on the altar.

I closed my eyes and started to meditate. Within seconds I was totally stoned, light-headed, dizzy, and crying hysterically.

First, I knew beyond a shadow of doubt that my stone had found the right home. The Krishna rock from Govardhan would be cared for and honored properly. And then there was the presence of Maharaji. It filled me and sent torrents of energy soaring through my body. The crying was most definitely a rush of joyfulness that I could not control in any way. After a length of time, I'm really not sure how long, I felt a gentle hand on my shoulder.

"Sruti Ram, it's time that you left now."

It was Ma's assistant and they were preparing to leave soon.

I feel that the whole Krishna experience was highlighted by my Maharaji experience in Ma's room. I believe that it was Maharaji's way of showing me his connection to Krishna and, ultimately, Ram—an example of yet another road, another tangent. The road to Govardhan brought me back to Lord Ramachandra—another acknowledgement of Divine presence influencing the journey.

The Divine makes himself known in so many ways, simply because he can. But we must acknowledge the state of grace we live in to become clued-in to the gifts that the universe presents to us as evidence that we are loved, protected, and guided by our existence in the power of love. Being positive brings positive energy to us.

CHAPTER 17

BOTH THE SAME

THE NEXT YEAR, 2008, I was in the foothills of the Himalayas during a glorious season. I had just made my pilgrimage to the mountain ashram in Kainchi and I was now getting settled. It was not an ideal time, as the ashram and temple were officially closed. But after I indignantly (I confess) refused to leave, the order came from Sri Siddhi Ma that I could stay.

Eventually, it came to pass that I was to be in charge of the Maharani's rose garden. The Maharani was an old-time devotee of Maharaji and was extremely close to Sri Ma.

I was allowed to visit with Sri Ma on a daily basis. While visiting with Sri Ma in a neighboring town, high in the Himalayas, she turned to me and asked, "What's wrong with you today, Sruti Ram? You don't look right to me. What has disturbed your mind today?"

I told her that I had ventured into Nainital, a neighboring town, to visit a cyber cafe and communicate with the folks back home in America. I received an email from my cousin in which I learned that my uncle was very sick. He had been a very good man all his life and it made me sad that he had to suffer so much now. Being so far away and not being able to comfort him was very distressing.

Ma closed her eyes for a moment, then instructed me to go into

Maharaji's room later that evening to meditate. She would be there and would meditate with me.

That evening I obediently went to Maharaji's room, sat in the corner on the floor and started to meditate. Slowly I felt the vibration in that glorious space change; the air seemed to get thick and warm. I opened my eyes, looked around the small room, and thought I saw someone sitting beside me.

Is it Sri Ma, I wondered? Why can't I see her clearly? I could feel that someone was there, so I satisfied myself with that cognition and continued to meditate. The room was like a container that was being filled from the bottom up with liquid energy pouring into it. I opened my eyes again and I could see who was sitting next to me: it was Maharaji. At first it startled me, but eventually the wonder of it all balanced out and comforted me. I was ecstatic over the visitation.

Eventually I focused my intention on my uncle and his healing. A great feeling of calm came over me and I was sure that something had been achieved successfully, although I did not know what. When I returned to my room, I tried to sleep but could not calm the ecstasy, so I continued to meditate until the sun came up. I felt completely rested when I went back to report to Sri Ma. The moment Ma saw me she commented on how much better I looked.

"I am feeling much better, Ma."

"Your uncle is a good man. And now he has no more pain."

I took her word as truth and felt at ease with the entire situation.

Later that same day, I went back to a cyber café and learned that my uncle had passed away as we were praying for him. I was told that his pain seemed to subside completely and that he was resting in peace before he died.

Who was in the room with me that night? Was it Maharaji? Was it Siddhi Ma? It didn't matter. It was proof to me that Siddhi Ma is imbued with his energy. He used to say that when he was remembered he would always be there. Maharaji was called for and he came as promised. No surprises there, but always a fantastic testimonial as to his influence in my blessed life.

He has never let me down.

After a few days had passed and I basked in the joy of illumination and grace and the simple fact that I was so blessed to have such a loving and magical time there in the mountains with the holder of the lineage, it was time once again to return to America.

On the last day of my visit with Sri Ma, we were sitting on the veranda of her mountain sanctuary and the moment was at hand for our goodbyes.

I sat before her on a blanket. She was accompanied by her life-long companion, Jivanti Ma.

I bowed forward to touch her foot with my hand and a small medallion that I wore around my neck slipped out from my shirt. Sri Ma noticed it and gently reached over and placed the hanging medal in her hands. She stared at it for a moment and then her face lit up. She then motioned to me to remove it from my neck.

"Maharaji!" she exclaimed. She caressed the silver medallion that was inscribed with the word *Ram* in Sanskrit. Holding it, she began to weep. She literally washed it with her tears.

Then she passed the medallion over to Jivanti Ma, who also held it in her cupped hands and began to weep. Bearing witness to this, I too began to weep.

You see, contained within this hollow medallion were the ashes of Maharaji. The ashes had been given to me by a pujari who had the responsibility to safeguard this treasure. I had never mentioned to anyone what was contained within it. It was my personal relic.

I told her that I felt so blessed and did not really want to leave. She instructed me to remember the joy and knowledge gained and take these feelings and share these impressions with the community back home. She appointed a young man to accompany me all the way back to New Delhi on the train. Soon after that I was back in the States, glowing with the light of love.

Grace is always available to us. It simply IS. You do not need to be in a special place to make contact with it; just be open and aware that it exists for all of us to make contact with.

CHAPTER 18

IT'S ALL ONE

B ACK IN WOODSTOCK, I spotted a crow in a bare tree just outside my window and remembered an encounter I'd had in India. It had been a beautiful day, bright and sunny. On these mild days, I had the habit of practicing yoga and meditation on the roof of a beautiful ashram located in Rishikesh. It offered a perfect view of the Ganges and the wildlife refuge across the river.

While I was doing my hatha yoga on the roof, a large black crow came to visit. Standing very nearby on the railing that surrounded the roof, the crow screeched at me. At first it seemed unusual that a crow would be so close, as crows are usually quite skittish around people. Also, it seemed evident that he was trying to tell me something.

I remained as calm as I could and pondered what the message could be. It dawned on me that if I were back in the States, I would be feeding the crows as part of my daily morning activities. There had been very heavy snowfalls near my home in Woodstock and I realized that the crows might be low on food. During the winter, it was a daily occurrence for me to literally call the birds with a whistle and they would soon appear in the trees above me, waiting for their daily rations.

This crow continued to talk to me for quite a while. When I got the message that I perceived he was formally delivering, he left. That day I emailed a friend and asked her to please purchase some seeds and go to my house every day to feed the crows. She agreed, and I told her that I would reimburse her when I returned.

Two days later, a crow—perhaps the same crow—returned to the roof in Rishikesh. This time, however, it had a full piece of sliced bread in its mouth. The crow hung out for a while, flaunting his breakfast, then left. I thought he was telling me that my crows back home were being fed. I felt the chore had been accomplished and was at peace. Some months later, when I returned to New York, I thanked the friend who had been feeding the crows and asked how much I owed her for the seed.

"Oh, that's okay," she responded. "I never actually spent any money on them. I just went to the health food store and asked them to give me their day-old bread so I could feed the crows. They agreed and gave me bread every day."

I was dumbfounded. She was feeding the crows sliced bread, and the crow on the roof was holding a piece of sliced bread. Coincidence? Perhaps! Magic? Definitely!

In the Hindu tradition, it is said that crows are reincarnated rishis, high priests. It is considered a blessing to feed them, and I did so with great pleasure. What kind of cosmic parallels I experienced, I don't really know for certain; I surely have a strong feeling about it, though.

Miracle after miracle, understanding the cohesive fabric of the universe leads to a comprehension of irresistible love, of our oneness with everything that is.

CHAPTER 19

NO ROOM FOR DOUBT

A T THE AGE of fifty-seven, I woke up one morning in my home in Woodstock with a big lump in my side. Apparently, I had a hernia. A double one. According to the doctor, I needed surgery; it was mandatory that it be repaired.

About a year before this incident, I had learned a very ancient healing mantra from one of my Indian teachers, who is a fabulous mystic and an enormous storehouse of ancient knowledge. It is a Shiva mantra and is used by just about every Indian to insure good health and healing. The fact remained that a surgery was still required, so I made the appropriate arrangements.

The interesting fact about this mantra is that, unlike others, it must be recited aloud. It is believed that the vibration created by the sound of the ancient Sanskrit words literally lays on you like a blanket. One repeats the sounds many times to increase the power of the vibration. It is so strong that it is not really necessary to recite it. A person can listen to a recording of the words and receive the benefits.

I made it clear to my doctor that I did not want to be put under during the operation. He protested, but I demanded that was how I wanted it to be done. On the morning of my surgery, I reported to the hospital as instructed. I had started repeating the mantra early that day and continued to repeat it softly as often as I could. I did get a lot of strange looks from people in the hospital as I was "singing" all through my admittance.

They wheeled me into surgery. The doctor greeted me and numbed the body parts in question, as I wanted to be able to sing the mantra. I lay on the table with a little curtain barrier in front of me so I could not really see anything going on, and they proceeded to do their work. Every once in a while, the doctor would peek over the curtain barrier and ask how I was doing; after the third time, I asked him, "Is everything okay? You keep asking if I'm all right. Is anything wrong?"

Looking at me over the curtain, the doctor responded immediately. "Besides the fact that this is a double hernia, here I stand with my hands in your guts and you are singing a song," he said. "It's very unusual."

"Oh no, doctor, I'm not singing a song. It's a healing mantra from India."

"Well, keep it up, my friend. I have never seen anything like it. Your blood pressure has not moved in the slightest. It's very steady and normal. Well done. I'm delighted."

He finished the operation and I volunteered to walk back to the recovery room.

"No," he said, "don't move off the table. I don't care how fit you feel, you must be wheeled to recovery."

In the recovery room, I asked to speak to the nurse, and he quickly came over. "What can I do for you, sir? Are you in pain?"

"Oh no, not at all," I told him. "I was wondering if I could go to the bathroom. I'm also very hungry. Any chance of getting a pizza in here?"

Apparently astonished by my request, my nurse called out to the other nurse, "Hey, Charlie, I have a fifty-seven-year-old male here who just had major surgery. He wants to take a pee and order a pizza. Do you think we can send him home?"

The other nurse smiled, agreed that I sounded just fine, and they dismissed me. My friend picked me up and drove me back home. I continued to repeat the mantra, and in two days I felt so fit and healed that I bought an airline ticket to New Mexico so I could attend a festival at the temple.

I am living proof of the power of that healing mantra. I often tell this story in my dharma talks, and I give that mantra to all who want it. Here it is:

Sruti Ram after singing at Mahakal Temple in Ujain, India, c. 2004. A red tilak painted on the forehead symbolizes the third eye.

> *Mahaa Mrityunjaya*
> *Om Triyambakam Yajaamahe*
> *Sugandhim Pushtivardhanam.*
> *Urvaarukamiva Bandhanaat*
> *Mrtyormuksheeya Maamrtaat*

The translation is: *We worship Lord Shiva, the three-eyed one, the one who is the master of all senses and qualities, and the one who is the sustainer of all growth. May he release us from the bondage of death as a ripened cucumber is released from its vine and may he grant us immortality.*

The mantra is saying that we don't ever die. Our bodies do. That's the essence of the whole mantra. It's to reestablish the belief that we will go on, whatever happens to our bodies. But it's renowned as a healing mantra of miraculous abilities, and I was the living proof of that. As we all know, especially those of us who have endured abdominal surgery, it can be very complicated. But this was radically different than any other surgery I'd ever had.

We are more than our bodies. And in time, we will drop our current body and continue on to yet another body. As this healing mantra asserts, our essence does not ever die.

CHAPTER 20

SITA AND RAMA WANT A CHANGE

O NE EVENING I went to bed after doing my evening puja and
prayers. I was very tired and looked forward to a good night's
sleep. It must have been about three o'clock in the morning when I
was awakened by a voice in the night calling my name—

"Sruti Ram—"

Startled, I sat up in bed. Must have been dreaming, I thought. It
was one of those times when the space between dreaming and wak-
ing seemed so unclear. I tried to sleep. A few moments later I was
aroused again by the voice calling me—

"Sruti Ram—"

This time I jumped up out of the bed. I was certain there was
someone in the house. I went downstairs feeling rather nervous and
fidgety.

"Who's there? Anybody there?"

No reply. After a thorough search, I went back upstairs. As I was
entering my room, the voice called my name once more. This time
it was evident that it was emanating from the room adjacent to my
bedroom—Sita and Rama's room. I had created a separate room for
them, as my teacher had instructed me to worship in private.

I slowly entered the room and sat before the images. Experiencing
a dialogue with the beloved images was not new to me. In fact, it was

one of the most rewarding aspects of the practice. I asked, "What would you have of me?"

"Sruti Ram, we want to be downstairs in the temple room. The time has come for us to give darshan, visitation to all who come to this house."

Very well, I thought. *I shall move them down there right now.* I was filled with a new energy and wasn't tired at all. This kind of interaction was always a delight for me. I started moving everything around in the temple room and made space for my beloveds. This went on for about three hours, as I paid attention to the requirements of Vedic traditions, following the guidelines of direction and spacing of the altars and such. Finally, feeling that all was right, and that the new additions were properly installed, I retired to my bed.

I was just entering the sleep mode, feeling very accomplished and secure that I had complied with my instructions, when I heard it again. *"Sruti Ram."* I proceeded directly to the temple room, bowed reverently, and asked the duo, "What is required, Lord?"

Ram replied immediately, "We are facing the wrong direction." I realized they were in fact not properly installed according to the Hindu rules. I had misinterpreted the traditional method. So, naturally, I redid the entire room, being even more attentive to the rules and regulations. It was now around seven in the morning and all seemed to be corrected in that small temple. Sita and Rama looked beautiful.

Since then, all who come to the temple have Sita Ram's darshan. What makes it even more fun for me is that a person does not even have to be a devotee or practitioner to receive the blessing. All that is required is that they see the images and that's it: they have got it! Of course, those who are looking for the blessing usually sit there for some time, soaking it up with great delight. Sita and Ram, Laxman and Hanuman reside in that same room to this very day. Many revered teachers and swamis have been in their presence since, and all remark about the power in that space.

With these sacred images of the Gods, we do not decorate to suit the room; we accommodate the Gods by changing the room to suit the flow of energy. This method of room arrangement, called *Vastu* in Sanskrit, is the equivalent of Chinese Feng Shui. Because of that night's restructuring, altars were also created for the Divine Mother and for Lord Shiva. It was a very busy evening.

When we open ourselves without question to the instructions of the Divine, everything falls into place—sometimes literally.

CHAPTER 21

REMEMBER ME

I WAS RETURNING home from a visit to my beloved Ram Dass in California, and after a wonderful two weeks at his home, I was filled with the spirit of love and community. My dear Baba had a very active and dynamic energy, and I felt honored to have been so loved and accepted by all the residents in that house.

I was offered a lift to the airport and arrived too early for my flight, which turned out to be a boon. During a very turbulent rain and electrical storm, an incoming plane had been struck by lightning and, consequently, many flights were either delayed or canceled.

My own flight was canceled, and the airline was able to get me on another flight, which was departing an hour earlier than my original flight. My layover in Chicago was longer than expected, but there was not much I could do about it. As I waited patiently, the delay was further extended. Instead of arriving in New York at 7:30 p.m., I would arrive at 2:30 in the morning, which would automatically void my ride from the airport to my house. I thought I would solve the problem by renting a car and driving myself home, but no rental cars were available. Okay, I thought, I'll go to a small hotel and have my friend pick me up in the daytime. But the airport hotel rates were totally out of line for even a simple room. I was stymied about what to do.

I stopped and collected my thoughts. Almost immediately, Maharaji was present in my mind. An internal conversation began: *So, Baba, you managed to get me this far safely and now I am in a rather difficult position. I am asking you to get me home tonight.*

No sooner had I finished the thoughts to my Baba when I felt a hand on my shoulder. "Excuse me, but you were on the same flight as I was," a strange voice spoke from behind me. This actually startled me, so I was dumbfounded by the solicitation of a complete stranger.

I turned around and tried to recognize the fellow. "You were in the airport in Chicago."

"Yes, that is correct. I remember you now."

"I see that there are no cars available for you."

"Right again."

"Well, I phoned ahead and reserved a car for myself. I think it was the last one."

"That seems to be the case," I replied with a slight edge.

"I'm driving north to Albany. Would that do you any good? You can ride with me if you like."

"Would you consider taking me to Woodstock?"

"Sure, that's no problem, as long as you can direct me back to the Thruway."

Wow! This was a pretty fantastic development.

This guy was one heck of a nice fellow and we laughed and chatted all the way to my front door like we were brothers or old friends.

Yet again, my Baba was there for me. I have found that Maharaji always keeps his word. I called on him for help and there he was, almost immediately. Over and over, this magic occurs and constantly reinforces my faith. He is always there; we just need to surrender to the higher power and get out of the way for the universe to serve us.

What we call coincidence may in fact be an act of faith that happens without any effort. Every problem has a solution, and even the mundane problems of everyday life can be solved by manifesting positive energy.

CHAPTER 22

GURU–THE FOUNTAIN OF GRACE

I HAVE A close friend who has become a famous kirtan singer. He travels around the world chanting the names of God. He was appearing near my home in Woodstock, and I decided to attend the kirtan. Upon my arrival, I received his usual friendly welcome and got a great seat directly in front of the performers.

Traveling with him on this leg of the tour was a female swami, also a singer. Her name was Ma Chetan Jyoti. She looked very interesting, all dressed in orange, and her intensity was fascinating. She was a white Canadian who had been traveling in India with her husband when she got the calling, and she had gotten divorced and moved to India permanently. She had been ordained as an Orissan Swami (from the province of Orissa; Orissan swamis are Krishna devotees) and lived there for about thirty years. She had established an ashram in Rishikesh and was well known throughout the area.

While we were waiting for the festivities to begin, I engaged her in conversation. "Where in Rishikesh do you live?"

"So, you know Rishikesh, do you?"

"Yes, I do. Actually, I have just returned from a journey there."

She described the location of her ashram on the banks of the Ganges. I knew exactly where it was, as I had resided nearby.

The devotee appears before an image of his guru, Neem Karoli Baba, in the ecstasy of kirtan.

"Do you sometimes play music and sing from the roof of your ashram?"

She could not mask her surprise. "Well, yes, I do."

I could see that she was now intrigued by my inquiry. I continued, "I would bathe in the Ganges every morning at the *ghat* just below your house, and you would be singing the praises of Krishna while I took my bath. The majesty of the river, the sense of community with all the many bathers and worshipers, and the joy of being in that sacred place in conjunction with your chanting was the most beautiful event of each morning."

Chetan Jyoti was delighted by this "coincidence" and wanted to pursue the details of that previous encounter. But this was not the right time and place for a lengthy chat. The moment had come for the singers to do their kirtan. They proceeded with their chanting and it was great. She had a beautiful voice and her devotional mood was outstanding and her devotion was exceptional.

After the concert I invited her to my home for a visit and some tea. Sometime later she complied with a phone call and eventually visited my home. We enjoyed chatting about mutual interests and quickly became good friends. We discussed many aspects of devotional practices and philosophies, many of which we both agreed on.

As a result, I invited her to return for a stay after her tour obligations were completed. She agreed and returned to my home to stay for a couple of months.

That time together was just wonderful. We shared more deeply personal stories about our lives and spiritual experiences in India. Most of all, I truly enjoyed doing daily kirtan together. It was joyful to sing with her. Through her expertise, Chetan Jyoti encouraged my voice and brought me to new realms of chanting and kirtan experience.

We soon discovered that we chanted beautifully together and started singing kirtan around town and in neighboring areas. We created a small center in town and had weekly teachings and kirtans there.

The local seekers were delighted, and these weekly meetings spawned lots of interest and questions about the practice of devotional chanting. After several months, her time in the West came to a close. Due to visa regulations and her responsibilities back home, Chetan Jyoti returned to India.

A connection that may seem random is often the seed of some greater purpose. We have only to listen and make room for what is indeed meant to be.

CHAPTER 23

THE PURPOSE IS DEVOTION

WHEN THE WINTER months rolled around in America's Northeast, I once again planned my next pilgrimage to India. Visiting my new swami friend Cheytan Jyoti was very much part of the plan. We reunited in Rishikesh and initiated our singing regimen immediately. We sang for one of my teachers, Sri Ma, in the Hanuman temple.

There were many wonderful months with Sri Ma in India. Due to Cheytan Jyoti constantly urging me to sing in the Hanuman temple, chanting had become a primary component of my daily practice. Very often, in a room full of Indian devotees, Ma would request that I sing the Hanuman Chaleesa. It was a long prayer and I was always concerned about proper pronunciation. For the most part, the Indian folks in attendance did not know this prayer and they would always be impressed that a Westerner had this ability. The sincerity of my intention, becoming one with the devotional mood, eradicated any egoistic fears.

If performance was the goal, I could not have complied with her instructions. But she knew devotion was my purpose. The Indian people had the ability to identify the element of *bhaav*, or spiritual intention and mood in my singing. The other surprising development was the radical change in my voice. It became stronger and more melodic every time I sang. I am sure that Sri Ma and Maharaji's grace created the voice I have today, another gift of love. My entire being embraced a sense of oneness with the divine energy promoted by this practice. I was quite at home with it all. Home is where the heart is and I knew I was absolutely in my heart.

Eventually we decided to make a *yatra* or pilgrimage to many sacred temples, and our singing became our gift to the deities that resided within those holy places. One remarkable experience of that tour was chanting in a place called Mahakal.

Sruti and Chetan Jyoti Ma in India.

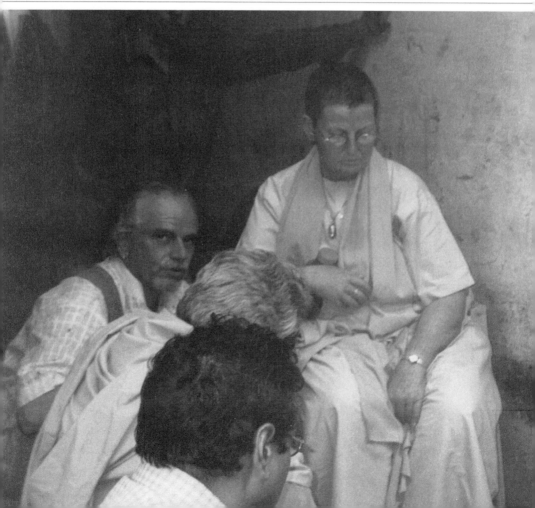

One of the oldest Shiva temples in all of India, it was located in the city of Ujjain in Central India. We arrived during Shivaratri, a major holiday, and this temple is the home of a Jyotirlinga. As legend has it, these types of lingam stones were self-manifested and are present in several locations around the world. As a matter of fact, "self-manifested" implies that the stone was present before the temple was built, and upon its discovery the building was erected around it.

We were invited to be the guests of honor at this colossal celebration, and we were extremely honored. That evening we appeared at the great temple. Seated on the stage with our traveling band of accomplished musicians, we were in awe of the immense crowd and the fervor of the assembly. The gathering was filled with high energy and excitement. Even the media was present: TV and newspaper reporters, along with dignitaries of various ranks.

Swami leaned over to me and asked, "How many people do you think are out there?" I looked out at the sea of faces and guessed there must have been at least five thousand in attendance.

There were many singers performing there that night, but we were highlighted as special guests. It was an unusual happening. First of all, we were not Indian. My friend was a female swami, originally from Canada, and I was an unknown devotee from America. The holiday itself was very important and the city of Ujjain is not a place where you see many white faces. You can't even cash a traveler's check there; only Indian money is acceptable.

We were as incongruous as Muslims singing rock music at St. Patrick's Cathedral on Christmas Eve.

Most of the kirtan sung that evening was in the contemporary style. It was a Bollywood type of music that was extremely popular throughout modern India. We, however, elected to sing a traditional Om Namah Shivaya kirtan. It doesn't get much more traditional than that. We thought it was a little risky to be rather old-fashioned, but we wanted to maintain a proper level of decorum. The fact of the matter was that we really were lovers of the old-fashioned traditional style.

We sang our hearts out that night. TV cameras and audio recordings were happening all about us, and the crowd seemed to love what we did. The energy was electric and people were dancing in the aisles and responding wholeheartedly and energetically.

After our part was complete, we stayed and enjoyed the celebration for a while. It was a gigantic holiday and the celebration would go on for many hours. We were exhilarated and blissful but tired. We then retired for the evening.

The next morning we set out on our daily walk and quickly became aware of our new popularity with the locals. It was a little surprising but very pleasant. Many people in the streets greeted us with friendly salutations and sincere respect. It seemed that we had been totally accepted overnight. One of our companions noticed a local newspaper for sale along our walking route.

Oh my God, there we were, on the front page. The headline read: *TRADITION RETURNS TO MAHAKAL FROM WESTERNERS.*

We were dumbfounded by this acceptance and compliment. We also discovered that there had been eighty thousand people in attendance that previous night. But then we discovered the real prize. Due to our choice of traditional kirtan, the Mahakal Temple officials determined that a new commission would be organized to jury the future kirtans. All music sung for the Shivaratri holiday at that temple would be traditional from that evening forward. What a great happening: Tradition was indeed returning to India from the West.

I had been told many years ago by one of my teachers that India was losing its spiritual essence because of the influence of Western materialism. He also believed that Indians' sudden interest in Western culture and acquisitive tendencies and Americans' surging, passionate practice of Eastern philosophy were in alignment. This lost spiritual essence would return to India through the Westerners.

Now I was a part of that. It was an extraordinary event. Doing kirtan in that ancient, sacred place of such importance with eighty thousand voices singing call-and-response back at us was more than I could ever have dreamed of doing. I thought it was the pinnacle of a public chanting experience. Dreams are of the mind, and this was far beyond the limits of dreaming to me. It was real.

I soon learned that these experiences would continue by the power of my guru's grace and my personal intensity of devotion to these customs and spiritual practices. Until then, I had not fully grasped the immensity of the guru's grace, or how comprehensive this gift would become in my life from that point forward.

When we pursue a dream from the heart with strong intention—not for the experience and ego gratification of performing, but out of a deep devotion—the possibilities are boundless. The power of grace is limitless and ever-present. Grace is always available to us; it is our natural birthright. I adhere to the concept that our practices enlighten our consciousness to the point that we recognize this blessing, which is available to everyone all the time.

The various disciplines help keep us focused and help keep our intention strong. Our teachers help us to attain a state that is our natural state of being, in which everything becomes possible. One event at a time develops into a path that leads to this realization. The practice of devotional love is an excellent way to manifest the good karmas of our lives, eradicate our dark karmas, and share the bliss of realization and liberation with each other.

CHAPTER 24

MORE GIFTS FROM HIM

D URING A VISIT to Vrindavan with my swami friend Cheytan Jyoti, we decided to go to Krishna's birthplace. Krishna was actually born in a prison cell in a town called Mathura. That building has since been transformed into a magnificent temple that today is one of the most popular pilgrimage sites in India.

Although the temple is massive in size, the actual cell is rather small—about ten feet by twenty feet. It has been reconfigured so that the sea of pilgrims and tourists enter on one side, pass through, and exit on the other. There is a rail running the length of the room and a priest is always present to safeguard the sanctity of the original site.

We entered that holy area, respectfully observed the space, and bowed to the images in residence according to the custom. We sat down and proceeded to chant. This is one of the most wonderful aspects of chanting in India. One can enter into just about any temple and start singing a devotional prayer or chant at any time.

The kirtan was ecstatic and we continued chanting for an unknown amount of time. With our eyes closed and our hearts open, we poured out the love and devotion we felt. It seemed we could sing forever. Cheytan and I alternated the leading positions and chanted together. It was a magical time out of time.

In spite of our devotional impetus, after an hour or two our voices became tired and our throats a little sore, so we concluded our devotional incantations.

Upon opening our eyes and slowly regaining our physical awareness, we noticed that the room was filled to capacity. With our eyes closed we were not aware that devotees and pilgrims had chosen not to pass through but to stay and join us in the bliss of the event. Unbeknownst to us, while we were singing, people were placing flower *malas* and garlands of flowers on and around us in gratitude and approval, as is the custom for people to show their appreciation on these occasions. We were overwhelmed with love and happiness when we realized what they had done.

The priests that attended the shrine came over to us and gave us prasad, or blessed food, and invited us to return frequently and sing again. This priest was noticeably joyful and so very hospitable.

The beauty of the shrine, the scent of the flowers, the looks of gratitude and approval, and the love of God that permeated our beings made this a platinum moment etched into my psyche forever.

This was the place where Lord Krishna was born, and here I was—a man from another country and culture—singing his name centuries later. Here I was accepted and honored and loved. All this had come as the result of searching for something in this life that could bring some peace and comfort to my soul. Phenomenal as it was, I knew I was home, and that my intention always to focus on the God element in life would bring more than ever anticipated. I now had much evidence that could substantiate and support my belief—so much more than I could have ever imagined.

Devotional love leads to self-realization and it's what makes the journey so much fun. I've learned so much about my personal process through joy. This was a major lesson. In the past, it seems to me, many of us have garnered teachings that the heart's opening comes from a place of suffering. I know that suffering opens one's heart, as when someone close to us dies and we think back on how lovely it was having them in our lives. However, the power of a joyful experience is even greater and creates an even more tangible and accessible reality for teaching and learning. It's the stuff that gives us the capacity to go on and share how we feel with each other and with the world. Now I was sure that the fog of ignorance could be replaced with positive clarity of knowing, and that the rewards would be greater than ever.

Through the intention to serve and love the Divinity within us, we manifest Divine energy. This devotional love is the way to self-realization and makes the journey full of joy. Many of us have received the lesson that suffering opens the heart, but the experience of joy is even more powerful. It's the stuff that makes us go on and share our feelings with each other and the world.

CHAPTER 25

THE ICING ON THE CAKE

I WAS STILL dependent on other musicians to play for me while I sang, and I wanted so much to enrich my personal devotional experience by being able to accompany myself. I was singing for the Gods, and that kind of seva has an inherent striving for perfection. It can always be better. There is always more you can do to improve.

When my visit to India came to an end, I made it a point to have a superior harmonium made for myself, crafted by one of India's premiere instrument makers. I carried it back to the United States and was determined to learn how to play. I tried for months and just could not seem to master the keyboard. I loved chanting with musicians to accompany me, but in my private moments I was determined to become more accomplished on the harmonium.

On a typical day in my temple at home, sitting with the murti of Maharaji in my temple room and praying to him, I once again petitioned my beloved master: "Dear Baba, I can't do this without your blessing. You, who have given me so much, please help me to do this so I can go further with my devotional practice. I just want to advance my devotional ability for the glory of God alone. It makes me feel so much closer to you. Please help me."

I tried again, and from that day on I started to play that harmonium with a greater confidence. It seemed as though I was born to

Sruti Ram at a performance with SRI Kirtan.

it, not as a traditional musician but in a totally individual way. It sounds like no one else, yet it is completely beautiful and melodic. A close musician friend of mine, discovering that I could suddenly play with some ease and style, commented that I was the only person he knew who could make that instrument sound like a concert organ.

Consequently, I now travel a great deal to sing and play in many temples and ashrams by invitation. The best aspect is that I can sing beautifully to God in private with music that matches my mood. Every time I sing in my temple at home, I am stunned and delighted by the guru's grace that has allowed me to chant and play with such ease and love. It is always ecstatic.

The ability to share the joy of that union with the Divine with so many people, is still a wonder and an obvious manifestation of *guru kripa,* or guru's grace.

I have the greatest guru one could hope for. He does give me everything. I am perpetually grateful. Not only did he enable me to play, but he also gifted me with the ability to repair the instrument. Upon returning from a trip with the harmonium, I noticed that the keys of the board had been totally rearranged and could not be used. I was extremely upset and baffled about what to do. There are no local people here to repair this sort of instrument. Again, I prayed to Maharaji. "Lord, I can't fix this, but I am sure that you can. So, let's do it." And it was repaired right there and then. In less than an hour, the machine was operationally perfect, and it has been repaired many times since then through his grace.

These events may seem mundane, but the miracle of grace touches every part of life, both large and small.

It's all a wonderful journey when we have the eyes to see and comprehend the true power behind all these events. This power is available to everyone.

No one will be denied the wonder of it all. We just have to remind ourselves that we are not the doers. Remember God as the root stimulus of all events in our lives.

We always have the power of free will. How we direct that power is our choice. I believe that is why a formal practice is required for advancement. Using the tried-and-true has its benefits. The other multitudinous paths are always available.

But my personal experience has been made more fruitful by adhering to the rules of an ancient system. I have no reason to doubt its effectiveness.

LETTING GO

O N THE INDIAN holiday of *Raksha Bandhan*, brothers and sisters traditionally tie a red string on each other's right wrist. The female gives her brother some sweets and the male, in turn, gives some token amount of money to his sister. This custom has evolved in modern times so that now nonrelated ladies and gents exchange the string, which symbolizes a union of hearts that promise to be there for each other in times of stress or trauma. It's a custom that is demonstratively heartfelt.

On one occasion of Raksha Bandhan and the full moon, I was invited to participate in a local chanting event. I was happy to participate and contribute the kirtan as part of the program. Upon arriving, I felt a strange energy present. It did not feel malevolent, but I did feel something unusual. Then again, it was the full moon and energies are always rather strange on those occasions.

Although this group was not the usual gathering and kirtan was new to most of them, the chanting went into high gear and the enthusiastic crowd seemed to be enjoying it. While chanting and playing the harmonium, I started to have difficulty holding on to the instrument. It seemed to be walking away from me. I would pull it back and continue, but soon it would start walking away again. It became a major distraction.

Imagine trying to play a piano on wheels; it was almost funny. The mood was wonderful and the crowd was really one with the mood, but I was having a lot of difficulty trying to manipulate the instrument into a comfortable position and have it stay put. I felt the energy shift, and I intuitively stopped playing the harmonium. I continued to chant, keeping the rhythm by clapping my hands. It seemed that we were being influenced by another very different energy. When I stopped playing the harmonium, whatever seemed to be opposing me relented and the disturbing force was neutralized.

Something unusual had occurred and we all knew it. The rest of the kirtan was delightful.

The next day I received a phone call from the person who had hosted the event. She was full of joy in her descriptions of the event and one aspect in particular. Many people had noticed the dancing harmonium. They were also aware of my letting it go and continuing onward with great ease and a sense of surrender, but still maintaining focus. She stated this was the turning point for many folks that night.

It reminded me of the teaching of letting go of circumstances that seem to be obstacles on our path. We then can continue onward successfully. The lesson is to successfully undertake the assigned task and accomplish it. Keep the intention and focus clear and continue on despite the apparent distraction.

My caller stated that many people present had put that lesson to work from that moment on. There was a general and immediate understanding of "letting it go" within the group.

There are many instances in life when we are distracted by circumstances or energies that seem to oppose the completion of our task. We must maintain our equilibrium, keep our focus, stay in our hearts, and have fun.

All will be well. *I have always believed the best way to teach is to be.*

We accomplish our task and serve others in this simple and effective mode.

The lessons we need are always present as we progress on our journey. When we are truly ourselves, we teach others to share our joy. Be aware that the simplest lesson has great and expansive influence on our understanding of how it all really works. There is often a valuable lesson to be learned in what appears to be a mundane happenstance. Maintaining a balance through a quiet, internal knowing gives us the opportunity to function, accomplish, and teach simultaneously. It is actually very important to acknowledge that maintaining our focus with a calm resolve and disciplined reaction can highlight the teachings hidden within the circumstance.

CHAPTER 27

UNITY

EARLY ONE MORNING, after doing my usual puja in my swami
friend Cheytan Jyoti's temple, I decided to take the small boat
and cross over to the other side of the Ganges river, accompanied
by my friend. Boating on the majestic Ganges is in itself a sort of
pilgrimage to a seeker like me; it was beautiful and exciting.

Upon arriving on the opposite sandy shore, my friend took a nap
while I chose to chant and sing to Lord Shiva. I was experiencing
a powerful feeling of deja vu. It seemed I had done that very same
thing on this same beach in a distant past life. I fabricated a Shiva
linga in the sand and ornamented it with leaves and other items that
seemed appropriate like shells collected from the beach and various
blooms from nearby bushes.

When it was complete, I chanted ancient Shiva mantras for about
an hour. Then I drifted into a deep meditative mood. I could feel
the sun on my body and the sand underneath. My body seemed to
disappear. Before long, I was feeling completely free of my physical form. I experienced a sensation of lightness or weightlessness.
A great heat rose up within me. While sustaining my position the
body shook and sweat flowed profusely.

Eventually I lost awareness of the body completely. I felt as though
I had become a glowing mass of light. This great light emanated

from within; I felt like a phosphorescent nebula. For the span of a time I experienced no mind, no body, no thoughts or desires.

My only comprehension was that I succeeded in attaining a unity with the sand, with the water, with the sunlight.

I became one with everything that existed in my world and beyond. My form was the entire universe. There was no separation from anything that ever existed. I was one with all humanity, every person, the nature of every thought of every person, animal, flower, and inanimate object. This state was bliss—immense joy and love and power.

I thought perhaps I would die right there on the spot but recognized that I was ultimately immortal in that state as well.

However, that thought process stopped the experience, and I slowly became my mortal self again. Nevertheless, I was as happy as a man could be. And deeply in awe of this gigantic cognition: I had just become God for that moment. I knew then I could never be the same again, because this knowledge of this revelation would never leave me. I felt supercharged and light as air, all-powerful. I felt as if I could manifest anything I could think of. And then the realization of the magnitude of what had happened struck me.

Wow, I was elated and spinning with an internal joy. At that time, I was delighted that I was on an empty, isolated beach and that my friend did not witness any of my "having some." It was a private moment.

Cheytan Jyoti eventually woke from her nap and was not aware of my experience. I did not share it with anybody for a long time. I had been granted a unique visitation with God for a moment out of time, in a place where there was no separation from the One. I wanted to experience it again, for a longer period of time. And eventually I was able to do just that.

Into the black hole of infinity is the best way for me to describe it.

I call it Unity. It's a place where there is no ego, no mind, no body, no self. Being everything and everybody and being nothing and nobody.

Looking back at the original event, I wonder if perhaps I had stayed out of my mind longer, it would have been even more intense and revealing. But thinking about what was happening during the experience had separated me from it. I had become a witness to the event rather than one with it. My ego had been afraid of losing power over the body, of actually dying. I needed to stop the experience in order to allow my body to survive.

In actuality, I think it was the *fear* of dying that interrupted the process. Since that time, the ego has become weaker and the experience longer and stronger.

Unity exists in a place where there is no mind, no ego, no body. When we are not stuck in these, we are part of everything that exists, and more. We are Divine. We must acknowledge the fact that who we are can never really die; only the body is susceptible to destruction and termination. We are not our bodies with souls. We are souls with bodies, and our true selves are indestructible and eternal.

Maharaji's words ring true again with a deeper understanding: "It's all One." Indeed!

CHAPTER 28

HAPPENSTANCE

ONE GLORIOUS AFTERNOON in Rishikesh, I was sunbathing on the ashram veranda when the bell at the front gate summoned my attention. Outside was a gathering of young men who were unknown to me, requesting a visit with my swami friend. I quickly roused her, and she accommodated this crowd by granting them entry and offering tea. Eventually we learned they were from a temple in Rajasthan. They had brought several boxes that contained stone murtis that had become damaged and discolored by age and ritual. Their intention was to "bury" them in the Ganges River.

This is a traditional ritual and a proper end for such items. The ashram was located directly on the banks of the river and my friend agreed to expedite their desire. We prepared the small boat and climbed aboard with the murtis in tow. Out in the middle of the river, we lit some incense and said prayers. The statues were reverently lowered into the depths of the river in a slow and extremely solemn ritual. Knowing that the deities had had a proper farewell, the young men returned to the ashram, where they joined us for tea. They were all content with their accomplishment as they returned to their automobile and slowly vanished down the road into the dusty afternoon.

Some months passed. Time seems to go by very slowly in India, but actually India eats months like cookies. Is it the unimportance of time in general in the collective Indian consciousness that perpetuates the illusion that it lingers in a leisurely fashion?

We decided to visit a friend of Swami's in the south, so we packed our gear and drove for days until we arrived in a beautiful rural agricultural area of Rajasthan, with endless vistas of yellow mustard flowers, cows in the fields, and peacocks darting about in trees and bushes and terraces. As beautiful as it was, we could not locate the residence of Swami's friend. We stopped to call his ashram. He said we were very close by and he would come to guide us. After a while, his car sped into the waiting area. Out stepped the large, round swami, sure of himself and powerful.

Swami Gopal was a very respected teacher and a Shaktipat yogi. He was well known for his many attributes, including the ability to transmit jolts of energy to his students at will for the purpose of the spiritual evolution of the devotee. It is commonly believed that these transmissions are very effective and speed one rapidly along the path of spiritual development.

As Swami Gopal came towards me, he looked at me in a rather unusual way, folded his hands and uttered the traditional greeting, *Namaste*, which means, "I honor the light within you." In other words: *I see you and the God who resides within.*

He stared deeply at me and I felt an immediate connection with him. He was a large guy, and I could easily have been intimidated merely by his presence, but he actually had the opposite effect on me. I really did feel as though we had met before, even though I knew that we had not. It was a comfortable introduction.

When we reached the ashram, he ushered me to a large, comfortable room. When we were in the room alone, he looked at me with his large watery eyes, folded his hands, and again said, "Namaste. I have found you again at last." He had recognized me as his older brother from a past life, and he would do anything to accommodate my needs. In that moment, I could feel the strength of his conviction and I felt the same way towards him. As odd as it was, I truly accepted that he was my brother.

Another amazing event occurred later that day, when I was introduced to his students. He had gathered his many students from the village so that we could be formally introduced. To my surprise, all the young men who arrived were familiar to me. Startled, I determined that these were the same young men who had come to the Rishikesh ashram with the images of the deities that we had laid to rest in the Ganges River. Having been introduced months before in Rishikesh, we immediately bonded now here in Kaithal, their home. It was a reunion of sorts. I was amazed and delighted to know some residents of this strange place. It definitely enhanced the familial aspect of being there.

In the course of my life, one of my main challenges has been a fear of being alone in my old age. I had spoken to Maharaji in my prayers many times about this concern. Being totally aware of his benevolent and generous nature, I was sure that he would take care of me in some way. At that time in my life I practiced many disciplines, one of which was to be celibate and consequently not looking to develop any romantic associations. Thus, the reasons for the possibility of being alone as I aged.

While I was sitting with Swami Gopal, he said, "There is something that you must know. You shall return to America someday; your life is there. But it is important to understand and remember that when you want to return to India, you must come here to live. You can stay for as long as you like. You can come for a month, a year, or you can come and stay forever. You are my older brother and I shall take care of you and it will not cost you a single rupee." He even later explained to me his intention of building me a house at the ashram, complete with air conditioning and all the possible comforts.

I hadn't told him about my anxiety of anything related to old-age loneliness. Only to Maharaji had I ever uttered a thought on that subject in my meditations.

Though I seriously doubted I would ever take him up on that benevolent gesture, the fact remained clear to me: Once again my beloved guru had provided a refuge and solution from a major fear. He always has all the bases covered, whether I know it or not. The object of the story is to have unshakable faith—the cure for all fears. He is always taking care of me.

He always comes through one hundred percent. As Maharaji is an incarnation of Hanuman, it is guaranteed that a seeker and devotee will be cared for by Hanuman himself. It is so stated in the Hanuman Chaleesa, a powerful prayer that, if chanted in truth, calls on Hanuman to protect all his devotees.

There are so many aspects of spiritual realization that we can never imagine. But when we are living in the energy of positive evolution, we participate and discover totally unknown events of mysterious circumstance. A stranger may indeed be a brother.

CHAPTER 29

JEWELS FOR GOD

I N THE SMALL country town of Woodstock, New York, where I
live, there is a wonderful Tibetan monastery. I have always had a
fascination with temples of any kind and found myself going there
many times during its construction and during the preparations for
the opening of the Buddha's eyes—a major event in the life of a temple, as it is the actual investing of a statue with the life force. This
particular Buddha was, at that time, the largest statue of this kind
in America. It is also the official seat of the Karmapa in the United
States.

One day while the temple practitioners were busy preparing the
building for this major event, whose rituals it would take many days
to perform, I wandered around the place as though it were my home.
I felt as though I belonged there, even though I was not a Buddhist.

I happened upon a door to a chamber and entered into a room
full of monks, including the abbot. I was taken aback by the holy
gathering and immediately excused myself for disturbing them.
Much to my surprise, I was invited in. It seemed that all the monks
were working feverishly to complete a special job. They were painting cloth with saffron, which they would later wrap around stacks
of prayers, turning them into brightly covered bricks that would
be placed alongside the Buddha statue and eventually find their

permanent home in huge, glass-and-wood, floor-to-ceiling cabinets in the main shrine room. I felt out of place but accepted their warm and friendly invitation to join in their sacred work.

I told them I was not a Buddhist practitioner, but that many years before the temple had been erected, I had participated in a ritual on these grounds—taking refuge with the visiting Karmapa at a Black Hat ceremony. I also had received a Buddhist name at that time. Witnessing the Black Hat ceremony is considered by Tibetan Buddhist practitioners to be an extremely auspicious event in one's life.

We worked together all day. I tried very hard to be as respectful as a novice could be. At the end of the day, I excused myself and tried to leave quietly, but I was invited by the abbot to return the next day. Delighted, I agreed to return. This went on for five days.

Upon completion of the joyful task, I once again begged my leave from the abbot. This time he spoke to me as an old friend. He suggested that I return one more time, but this time I should bring some "treasure" with me.

What did that mean, I inquired?

"Something of value, perhaps some gold or a gemstone of some kind," he said. I thought that perhaps it was some kind of payment due to him for the honor of participating in the work.

Obediently, I returned the next day with a small emerald, a pearl, and a small bar of gold. He was delighted with my treasures and instructed me to wrap the jewels in a piece of paper with my name on it. I inscribed my name and my mother's name on two slips of paper and gave them to him. He then informed me that these gifts would be placed in a secret place in the altar and that I would be the recipient of continuous benefits generated by all the rituals that took place in that temple for all time. I was overwhelmed by the good fortune accrued by my devout and joyous efforts. I remembered the ceremony when I had been given a name by the Karmapa, which translated to "a life of auspicious fulfillment." How appropriate the entire scenario was and how magical the event came to be!

I never really could differentiate between the different forms of devotion, and this was another example of how a devotional heart focused on the glory of Divinity has many rewards. I think it's the element of innocence and respect for the form being worshiped that is the important factor. Honoring God is the definitive and always demonstrative aspect of my life, and it has always brought blessing and wonder to my existence. It made me speculate how many lifetimes I had been with those monks and what other wonderful projects we had accomplished together. Until this day, some forty years later, I have continued to wander through the temple, and I still feel completely at home in that sacred environment.

Since that time, the new Karmapa has visited our town at the temple many times, and he always seems like an old friend returning home.

When we live in harmony with people, places, and events, miracles and boons occur. Situations that are not even in our intentions can spring up and bless our present moments and even our future. So many secrets of the universe are presented to us in our everyday lives and environment. If we can be open to the magic of love and the power contained in that universal energy, only goodness prevails.

CHAPTER 30

KARUNAMAYI MA

KARUNAMAYI MA IS a well-known and respected Indian saint. She makes a world tour every year, and Woodstock is one of her favorite places to visit. Her programs start with a triumphant arrival to the Bearsville Theater to the sounds of a roaring kirtan from the crowd.

We, SRI Kirtan, are usually the singers for this part of the program. When Karunamayi Ma's 2014 schedule was posted, we were once again invited to participate in the same capacity we have performed for the last five years.

On the morning of June 2, we set up, had the usual sound check, and proceeded to do the warmup kirtan with the assembly. After a few mistaken arrivals, Karunamayi Ma finally arrived. We were singing our hearts out with the crowd, and her entry was jubilant and exciting. The Divine Mother took her usual place up on the dais and we brought the kirtan down to a slow gentle finale.

Usually at this point Mother would ask us to sing one more, and we would comply gratefully. It is always a pleasure and honor to be in this position. However, this time was notably different. After each kirtan, Mother would glance over at us, smile and say, "Sing one more, son."

Wonderful, yes, but this continued for two hours. She just wanted more and more from us. There were other singers scheduled, but they all had to wait until Mother stopped requesting more.

We finally reached the place we just had to rest our voices and bodies.

Originally, I had a scheduled doctor's appointment an hour away. I needed to leave the gathering by a designated time. When the two-hour timespan was becoming evident, I called the doctor and cancelled my appointment there, arranging a time three weeks later.

During these lectures and blessings, part of the program is to get in line and proceed one by one up to Mother for a private moment and personal blessing from her. As I stood in front of her, she looked deeply into my heart, a penetrating but lovingly powerful stare. Then she made the most remarkable statement to me.

"Sruti Ram, you know you are my son."

"Yes, Mother, I know, we are all your children."

"No, Sruti Ram, you are my son. Understand, you are really my son."

I was flabbergasted. Energy coursed through my body and she continued to shower me with gifts. She put a jeweled chain around my neck. Then she placed a shawl on my shoulder.

Marking my forehead with sacred powder, she sent for a picture of herself in which she was posed with Lord Shiva. And then came lots and lots of chocolate kisses. All the while this was happening, my eyes flooded with copious amounts of tears of gratitude and acknowledgement. "You deserve it, son. You deserve it, son." I responded with a sobbing thank you, and then she informed me that she wanted me to stay for the day. I was not to leave the building. I informed her that I had cancelled my doctor's appointment. I had waited two months for that appointment, but no matter. She waved it all off as an irrelevance and reiterated, "Stay the entire day." I did not totally understand, but I had the premonition that I was

Sruti Ram receives a blessing from the Divine Feminine, Sri Karunamayi, during one of her annual visits to her followers in Woodstock, New York.

being saved from some other less desirable happenstance. In about an hour I got a phone call from the doctor's office, rescheduling my recently made appointment to just a few days later. It was all too funny and lovely.

The person in charge of the day's event is a personal friend of mine. I related to her what Mother had said to me about actually being my mother. She responded, "Why are you surprised? Don't you remember what Mother said to you when you met her for the first time about ten years ago?"

"Not really," I responded. "What did she say?"

"Well, I was standing right there when she met you, looked into your eyes and said, 'Oh, my son, I have found you again. You have come back to me.'"

That statement had translated to me as a kind and loving but generic statement. But now the connotation was supercharged and extremely relevant to my journey. It was a recognition of another past-life incarnation and a glorious boost to my self worth. I was intoxicated with divine love and spent the rest of the day reeling over the adventurous episode of this day. It was a great day in the life of a seeker and lover of the Divine.

Blessed and empowered, I continue on my path feeling totally loved and protected.

During one of Sri Karunamayi's annual visits to Woodstock, Sruti Ram welcomed her to his home.

Offer your heart to God and remain dedicated to compassion and service. This is the true path to infinite correlation and ongoing bliss.

CHAPTER 31

I BELIEVE IN CHRISTMAS

IMMEDIATELY FOLLOWING THE traditional American holiday of Thanksgiving in 2013, I started to think about the next celebration of Christmas. I have always enjoyed these festive observances and really love the decorating and the creative endeavors surrounding them.

I decided that a large lighted tree out in the dark meadow outside my window would look wonderfully magical. However, I did not want to take down one of my own trees. I decided to go to one of the places in the nearby city of Kingston that sold precut trees for the season.

On one of many visits to Kingston, I went to a large nursery where I knew the selection would be extensive and beautiful. As expected, there were many trees to choose from.

Sruti Ram with his cousin Judi Purcell on Christmas Day, 1954.

The person in charge of sales promptly appeared to assist me and together we perused the collection of trees carefully until I found the perfect one.

Upon hearing it cost a prohibitive $350, I elected to leave without the beautiful but enormous tree. But I marked the tag on the tree with the word RAM so I would be able to find it again in the event that I weakened and decided to come back for it. After all, I still had plenty of time to pursue my dream tree elsewhere, but I had invested a lot of time in finding this one.

As time went by, the holiday drew closer. Still obsessed with putting a tree out in the field, I once again proceeded to Kingston. By now, two weeks before the holiday, I was getting antsy about the completion of my idea.

When I travel to nearby destinations, I usually choose the back roads, as the views are always more picturesque. Riding through a small community on a lovely slow road, I noticed an old man dressed in white pedaling a bicycle along the side of the road. It seemed rather strange to me. First of all, he was dressed entirely in white. White pants, white jacket, white hat, white shoes. It was a cold day and the weather was not conducive to a bike ride. The entire scenario seemed peculiar.

I deliberately slowed down as I cruised by to get a good look at him. As I passed him, I lowered my window so as not to distort my view. He turned his head as I drove past, and shouted at me, "Boy Scouts, Boy Scouts," and then turned away.

Thinking how strange this was, I slowed down for another look. The same drama occurred, but this time I noted that he looked familiar. Now rolling faster than he was pedaling, I looked up at my rearview mirror to see him again and he was nowhere in sight. I stopped and waited for him to return into view, but he was not there. He was gone. Vanished.

Sitting there on the side of the road, I ran the whole "movie" over in my mind. Suddenly it came to me. Holy smokes, that was Maharaji, my Guru. He had just appeared to me and shouted, "Boy Scouts." What the heck was that?

Then, in an instant, I remembered that the Boy Scouts sold Christmas trees for the holiday, donating the proceeds to charity.

Still confused by the visitation and what the meaning of it might be, I continued on my quest for a tree. Of course, I went straight to the Boy Scouts place.

Upon arriving, I got in line with some other folks and waited for some assistance. While I was standing in line, the man in front of me started a conversation. "Isn't it terrible, what happened here last night?" He told me that some people had sneaked into the lot and stolen about thirty trees. I was shocked and saddened by the report. He then informed me that several of the local nurseries had donated trees to the Boy Scouts to make up the difference. Smiling, we both agreed that it was all okay in the end.

Finally, a gentleman approached me and inquired what was I looking for. I asked if he had any really large trees. He stated that they had only one, which had just come in. We proceeded to its location, and there it was: the perfect tree.

"How much is that tree?" I inquired. He looked at me doubtfully. Then I noticed that the tree had a price tag on it. It said $350 but it was marked down to $75. Underneath the price was the word *RAM*.

Suddenly it all made sense to me. With a smile, I barked, "I'm not going to give you seventy-five dollars for this tree."

He looked back and said, "I know it's expensive."

"I'm going to give you $108 for it," I said. One hundred and eight is a powerful mystical number, especially for Hindus.

"Really?" he said. "Wow, that's great. Merry Christmas."

We were both delighted with the exchange and proceeded to

mount the giant tree on top of my small car. I was so happy to be there, and everyone present seemed so celebratory and "in the spirit." Driving home ever so slowly, smiling and chanting Jai Shree Ram all the way back to the field, I was electrified and totally hyper.

The magic and shakti, energy, of the total experience was almost overwhelming. That tree, standing out there illuminated in the darkness of the field, was stupendous and totally unforgettable. After all, I had his blessing, I'd experienced his visitation, and I was more than casually aware of his presence in my holiday and in my life. The great ones move in strange ways and it always proves to be rewarding to listen to the instructions given, while doing good and righteous work for the good of all.

My neighbors, friends, and everyone else who viewed the giant tree enjoyed the story and the blessings contained within it. It really was a very Merry Christmas.

Be open to blessings. They are everywhere, and hardly ever expected.

CHAPTER 32

WORSHIP OF THE GURU

I HAD THE honor to be with the Dalai Lama for three days, absorbing his lengthy discourses on love and how important it is. The situation was the grand opening of a temple in a nearby town. It was a large celebration and very important to the local practitioners. After a few days of various rituals, lectures, and gatherings, the moment came for questions and answers. I asked him, "Your Holiness, in all honesty, can you tell me that you really love the Chinese?" I am sure that to the assembly present, this was a very delicate inquiry and could possibly put the Dali Lama on the spot.

He became quiet for a moment, and then replied, "Yes! I can tell you in all honesty that I do love the Chinese. I view them as beloved family members who are behaving very badly." Tears formed in his eyes, and everyone present could feel the genuine emotion of his response.

I was struck by what an incredible teacher and being he is! The equanimity of his power and actions and how he responded to that terrible situation in Tibet was profound.

The Dalai Lama is obviously in communion with his soul. Our lesson from him is to elevate our own consciousness so that the world at large is elevated and change can occur. We all have the ability to be in communion with our higher self; nothing is more important than communion with our souls. Through the devotional practices of *japa* (the repetition of the name of God as a mantra on our beads), kirtan, prayer, meditation, and yoga, we can always remember the bigger picture.

One of the most important ways to participate in devotional practices is to have a guru or teacher. In the body or not, the guru guides us. He or she leaves us signs, like books, disciples, or lineage holders, which aid us in maintaining constant awareness in our endeavors. We must keep our perspective clear: we are each a soul with a body, not a body with a soul. Through devotional practices, we become more awakened to the fact that we are all one in the great unity of souls. When we are awake, it becomes more difficult to go back to who we were as separate egos. Once we are really awakened it is mostly impossible to return to the sleep of ignorance and nonaction.

Viewing the guru as a manifestation of pure consciousness allows us to go into the world of equanimity, beyond cultural boundaries, personalities, or gender. The guru is the embodiment of pure consciousness and is present within us as well.

Knowing that we also contain pure consciousness all the time is a primary realization. Maharaji would say, "Remember God, love everybody, see God in everything, and don't try to figure it out." It works, really!!!

In India, two types of gurus are recognized: an *upa guru* shows us the way, like a good teacher, while a *sat guru* IS the way. We can have many upa gurus, but we can belong to only one sat guru who is free of all worldly attachments and desires. The sat guru is recognized as salvation for the devotee. It's important to know that a person can be a wise upa guru, a pundit full of knowledge, but if that person is asking for donations or makes what seem to be ridiculous demands on us, then don't think this is your sat guru. Maharaji had only a blanket and would give even that away.

There is a phrase that represents the right relationship to the guru: "Taking the dust from the lotus feet of the guru and cleaning the mirror of our minds." Touching our head with that sacred substance indicates a desire to follow in the guru's footsteps—taking the dust from all those sacred journeys and paths they followed to arrive at divine union. We put it to our heads to illuminate our mind so we can bridge our mind to our heart and soul.

The kingdom of God is in the heart of every one of us. It's difficult not to change when we believe this. We don't have to escape from the world in order to change. We must simply do our duty and be responsible to our families, society, and our country. We do the best we can and let our higher selves guide us. In this way, we can become selfless, change our attitude to joyfulness, find a place of peace inside, and still be aware of what needs to be done no matter what the situation may be.

The guru takes care of us in so many ways. I have had the opportunity on many occasions to visit one of my teachers when he was in residence at the ashram. On one such occasion, I was invited to have afternoon tea. I groomed myself, dressed in proper attire, and went to his room, but the door was locked and the room was empty. This behavior was not typical of my very astute teacher.

I went to another room, where I found an assembly of the elder Indian devotees, among them my teacher. When they noticed me standing in the doorway, they immediately invited me in and gave me a place which would enable me to participate in the discussion. The conversation immediately changed to English as a show of respect for me, and my appreciation for all these considerations was apparent to them. After sitting there for some time, just listening, I finally interjected myself into the forum.

"Gentlemen, I have been considering asking you for some help. I have a specific problem, and I would like your counsel. Would you help me, please?"

I had the attention of all in the room. I explained my dilemma: "Maharaji is my guru. He gives me everything that I really need and has never let me down. I have a comfortable life. Every day I sing to him, cook for him, and try to live a dharmic life as best I can. Since I believe that he gives me what I need, yet I am still alone, perhaps having a partner is not good for me. However, sometimes I get very lonely. Can you help me with this problem?"

My teacher, Gurudat, rose from his chair and stood facing me directly, his arm outstretched with his index finger pointing at me. With that action, it seemed as though a golden brick of light came hurling at me and struck me between the eyes.

"You don't really believe that Maharaji is always with you. If you did, you could never be lonely."

I was flabbergasted by his demonstrative reaction. He was correct, of course.

It wasn't until that moment that I understood my loneliness was a lapse of faith and nothing more. My mind was spinning with delight as my dilemma had been instantly solved.

Remembering that Maharaji is always present, that I am never separate from him, was the exact medicine for my illness. I have since watched my mind try to return to loneliness, but the cure always kicks in to alleviate the suffering.

It's the ego, my mind and not my soul, that suffers that kind of malady. Maharaji is my constant companion and provider.

Doubt cannot be victorious when faith is engaged. Since that experience with Gurudat, I have never been lonely again.

We can all have very profound and exceptional experiences on this path with the guru. We do not worship the individual but honor the principles that he or she has lived by. Love, understanding, and compassion for all living things are principles that serve all.

Everyone benefits from this. It is our major contribution to our world. The cognition of a supreme element of divinity is what we receive when we worship the guru. With this intention, we are worshiping that aspect of ourselves that we recognize in that being. That very same aspect lies dormant in us—the true guru within.

Our personal experiences are unique, like no one else's. When we share these personal experiences, they start falling into the collective mix, the dynamic becomes enormous, and a fabulous new paradigm is generated. And we are an integral part of it.

Devotional love is the key. To tap into that balanced energy is to be in the place where we know that no matter what life throws at us, or what our karmas throw at us, we can deal with it in a conscious way, and then pass on. That's pass on, not pass away. Our time in the body, including all our troubles, is temporary.

We are perfect in the light of our soul. We are all precious jewels of ecstatic bliss, incarnated in bodies. We are not our minds or anything that our brains can conjure up. If we learn to serve each other from an egoless place, we can complete the liberation of our mind and be totally fulfilled.

Being fulfilled is having an abundance of passion for the truth, to manifest within ourselves and to expedite that energy in everyone who touches our lives. If we serve each other in that way, we are walking the walk. If we just simplify our ideas of how to live honestly and compassionately, we make a major contribution to the quantum leap that is our birthright, to higher consciousness for humanity.

CHAPTER 33

BHAKTI

ACCORDING TO VEDIC philosophy, we are now living in an age called the *Kali Yuga*—a time of stress and difficulty.

It is written in the Shrimad Bhagavad that the smallest act of devotion in this age will reap large rewards simply because it is so difficult to be devotional now and to perpetuate a spiritual consciousness.

The benefit of devotion in this age is priceless. Through devotion, bhakti, we become aware of the state of grace that is actually our natural state of being. I often bring to mind the state of a healthy newborn baby. The purity of innocence is all a baby knows. Babies are open and vulnerable.

Love of God directs the mind to positive energy. When we come to know pure love through devotional practices, we eventually live effortlessly in our hearts, the place where all noble thoughts originate. Bhakti centers us in our hearts. Practice really does make perfect. Our actions and the fruits of our actions will display the joyful changes in our lives. We don't have to suffer to make ourselves change. All these delightful efforts support the journey to return to the source of all joy—the soul.

Living in a state of awareness is conducive to claiming the joy that is our privilege. We originated from the blissful energy of creation and we always have it in us. It's what we are really made of. Grace is our natural state of being, and devotion is one way to access the seed energy of joy contained within.

There is no need to constantly assess our self-development or to take this process to great lengths. Just feel secure in knowing that we are enjoying a state of grace that is always accessible and present for our evolution.

As we secure a place in our consciousness with heartfelt joy, we are able to be more powerful in our daily lives, and our prayers become extremely potent. Then we face the dilemma of being very discerning about what we pray for. Prayers to bring mundane results, such as wealth or other worldly concerns, are short-lived. I jokingly refer to this state as the "if-only syndrome." If we have higher prayers that benefit all humanity, prayers that attempt to change situations of great enormity in the world, then everything in our personal realm falls into place as well. We keep making deposits into that cosmic bank account. I believe that every time we chant the names of God, we are enlarging the balance in that account, allowing other people to make withdrawals to accommodate their needs. When we sing the chants, we join the great collective of all those who have sung before us.

The world of sound is infinite. Sounds travel the universe forever. Take a moment to fathom the enormity of that collective. That alone is enough reason to feel the joy of spiritual, not religious, community.

One of the ways I've learned about devotion is through contact with the images and stories of the Hindu gods. There is a wonderful and enlightening story called the Ramayana. In this extraordinary text, the trials and tribulations of Ram, Sita, Laxman, and Hanuman are highlighted and explained. The Ramayana's most profound chapter is the "Sundara Kanda." Maharaji once said that all the answers to living a good life are in that chapter. I highly recommend reading this literary masterpiece.

I think of these deities as aspects of our higher self. I like starting at the top; by being a devotee of Hanuman, I believe I am serving the president of the company. Hanuman, who is pure devotion, serves Lord Rama, who is the manifestation of pure consciousness; Sita, the wife of Rama, represents pure nature; and Laxman, Rama's brother, represents goals and accomplishments. These characters are all present in the Ramayana, along with the villain, Ravana, who represents the ego. His fierce form has ten heads, which represent the senses and the failings of the ego. Before he was a tyrant, Ravana was a great *sadhu* or priest practitioner. Through his austerities, he acquired tremendous power and was granted the boon of immortality by the gods. He became so powerful that eventually even the gods could not control him.

The development of *siddhis*, or powers, is not the goal of devotional practices. Powers are a trap or pitfall. In the Ramayana, Ravana wants Sita for himself—ego wants to steal pure nature from pure consciousness. In a timely fashion, pure consciousness (Ram) sets off to rescue pure nature (Sita) from the power of ego (Ravana). Devotion (Hanuman) assists Ram in his quest. In other words, we can rescue our own pure nature from the ego and the world with pure consciousness, pure devotion, high goals and determination.

Hence, we become aware of our soul's purpose through the images and story of Ram, Sita, Hanuman, and Laxman.

Rama dwells within us as our purest consciousness. Through our devotional efforts and the realization of higher goals, Ram and Sita are reunited.

We have many types of personality traits within us, devoted to different aspects of our lives: mental processes and the intellect; our karmic situations; the heart and compassion. I think that most of us who are aware of this truth really want to live in our hearts and originate all our thoughts and actions from there.

One of the main devotional practices to center us in our hearts is the repetition of the names of God as a mantra on our beads—the practice of japa—while staying centered on that divine form. Remember, it's not the personality we are embracing as we repeat the name of Ram, but the pure consciousness that Lord Rama represents.

If we surrender to the higher power and enjoy these practices that bridge that heart and mind, we are transformed. We won't change our minds; we will actually change ourselves. Mantric sounds readjust our vibrations and our intention readjusts our thinking. The deeper we go, the more vibrations build. For instance, most Hindu mantras begin with OM—a word that is believed to be the sound of creation. Hence the start and finish of each mantra is formed from, and returned to, the essence of creation.

Another devotional practice is called *arti*. We place the arti lamp in front of our beloved in a ritual of offering the light back to its source. The flame burns from *ghee*, clarified butter with all its impurities removed. It represents the purity of our souls. We offer it to the deity or guru who represents the culmination of everything we want to be. They have accomplished what we are aiming for. We offer our purity to the ultimate purity in order to become united with the great oneness of all. Then we take the light we have offered and bathe ourselves in it. This is accomplished by waving our hand over the flame as though we are beckoning the light to enter our bodies and minds. We imagine the sacred light illuminating and covering our entire being. We become closer to perfection and purity than before. It's our bath of fire for the day.

We must remember this unity during the day and empower ourselves all day long, knowing we have visited the spotless purity of our souls. As the old Harry Dixon Loes gospel song goes: "This little light of mine, I'm gonna let it shine."

In the Ramayana, Ravana, the demon king, became so powerful that he imagined himself to be the center of the universe. The ego can bring us great rewards and accomplishments, or ruination. We have seen it over and over again. These traits are recognizable in the great egocentric personalities in humanity's history. Ravana ruined his own life, and history has proven the same end for the lives of many people and nations who lose sight of the higher goals of leadership and power. Societies have disappeared because of the behavior of their leaders.

We need to feed each other with the nectar of love, not try to control each other. We can do that with compassion, praise, helpful words and ideas, and solutions for people's problems. It helps to be in the company of like-minded people, called satsang—the fellowship of those on the path. It's much easier to live consciously when you are supported by a group. That's why we must do a practice. The energy generated by these devotional disciplines will draw spiritual comrades to you. We must honor our incarnation and do our duty in the world. However, we can maintain balance through devotion, which links our heart and soul and helps us to enjoy the journey. It does not have to be a complicated ritual either. Imagine how different the world would be if we just give each other a compliment or helping hand every day. A simple kindness of acknowledgment for just being seen and appreciated can be a miracle in a person's life.

Better yet, we can just be the energy we want to see in our world and share it with everybody. We can share it even with people we don't like, knowing that we must love each other. We can move people out of our lives but never out of our hearts. An open heart is the responsibility of all awakened beings.

I like to think of the moving sidewalks in airports as being similar to the way we are all moving through our journey of life. We step onto the walkway and move rapidly through various situations. Through conscious awareness, we can take some strides while on that walkway no matter how fast or slowly it is moving. Spiritual practices, like meditation, doing mantra, or chanting the names of God, enable us to take those steps more consciously and move along even faster. We are still going in the same direction, but at the speed of light.

One of the simple things I do is to always have a kirtan CD on in my car while I'm driving. If there is a sudden accident, and it turns out to be my last journey, I want the Holy Names to be the last thing I hear as I travel on my way home. I use a similar technique in my quiet moments. I am always thinking of a mantra while doing any mundane activity as well.

I find that this being-in-mantra practice enhances the result of any daily program.

Devotional love is not a discipline. It is a way of living. Love and let live. This is the most conscious choice we can make and enjoy.

CHAPTER 34

THE HANUMAN CHALEESA

FOR ME, THE Hanuman Chaleesa, a prayer of forty verses about the powers and exceptional qualities of Hanuman, is an extraordinarily powerful devotional practice. Hanuman is the embodiment of giving—obedient, generous, and proper in every way. He illuminates the road to heavenly bliss through selfless service. While engrossed in obedience to Ram, Hanuman is always kind, benevolent, and uplifting in all actions and words. He serves without ego—and he shows us how to do it and consequently demonstrates the ecstasy and benefits of doing so.

Using Hanuman as a model, we become more aware of our own sacredness and our enormous power to accomplish just about anything the world can throw at us. Like Hanuman, we can acknowledge our position in life and our accomplishments, and always choose to serve others. To know that we are sustaining a balance in this way is true humility, and there is great power in humility. If we remain compassionate in our power, we advance all humanity.

Hanuman's ego is nonexistent. He does his appointed tasks for the glory of God and helps those who need to be reminded of their own greatness. We recite this prayer, the Hanuman Chaleesa, to remind him of how powerful he is. In the moment of his recognition of that greatness, he is unconquerable. In his Lord's service, he never thinks about how great he is himself. After the task is completed, he returns to his ageless posture of service.

Hanuman's monkey form exemplifies his humility. Choosing a form that is lesser than human when, as an incarnation of Shiva, he could have made himself magnificent, enabled him to serve his Lord Ram.

In the Chaleesa, we ask for strength, wisdom, and knowledge, and we petition to be free from impurities. The Hanuman Chaleesa is endowed with a siddhi, the power to alleviate the tensions of everyday life. One of the miracles of chanting this prayer is the way it purifies the mind—eradicating malice, fear of death, and ignorance, and helping to eliminate desire, greed, jealousy, and such. We can do that if we are honest in our intention and honest in accepting our failings. Hanuman holds a mace called a *vajra*, symbol of the lightning bolt of truth—a weapon that makes him unconquerable.

Hanuman takes delight in hearing the stories of Ram. This is another example of how pure consciousness is supported by devotion. We should take delight in reading about the realized ones and what they have done in their lives, which supports us in our

Lord Hanuman bringing Ram's ring to Sita, as stated in the story of Ram. Painting by Lakshmi (Christine) Tiernan.

endeavors to attain enlightenment. Taking delight in these stories is like sipping nectar on the path, filling the mind with images and thoughts of divinity. We can flood our minds with these vibrations.

Hanuman assumed many forms in the Ramayana. When Sita was captured and held prisoner in Lanka, Hanuman wanted to make it known to her that he was there and had a message for her. As the story goes, he made himself very small and hid in a tree. Pure devotion did not want to let his presence be known in the land of ego. As powerful as he was, he kept his form very small. After informing Sita that Lord Ram would save her, Hanuman grew to an enormous size and set fire to the land of the demons of ego, showing us how devotion can become the fire of purification. In his ability to be as large as a giant or as tiny as a fly, Hanuman shows us the balance of dharmic action acquired through devotional practice.

In the Ramayana, Lord Rama praised Hanuman, saying, "You are as dear to me as my brother Bharat." Here, pure consciousness is referring to his brother Bharat, who represents the aspect of duty and selflessness.

In the story, when Rama, Sita, and Laxman went into exile in the forest, Bharat was left behind to rule the kingdom. While consciousness and nature were in exile, the personification of duty governed. But Bharat refused to sit on the throne; he put Rama's sandals on the royal seat so Ram could step back into them when he returned.

During the great battle with Ravana, Rama's brother Laxman was mortally wounded. Laxman represents goals and determination, so goals and determination were wounded by the ego. Rama was distraught and ordered Hanuman to fly to the mountain where the life-giving herb grew, so he could revive Laxman. Hanuman, unable to determine which herb it was, brought back the entire mountain, and Laxman recovered. In this instance, pure consciousness depended on pure devotion to restore goals and determination from losses created by the ego.

Hanuman, son of the wind, embodiment of all blessings, removed all unhappiness by the root.

This line from the Hanuman Chaleesa acknowledges the presence of a higher power, the embodiment of pure devotion, and tells us that through pure devotion we can attain true fulfillment and happiness.

I purify the mirror of my mind and bow to the glory of Ram, who represents pure consciousness. He will bestow on us all the fruits of life. I know I am ignorant, so I remember you, Son of the Wind, the very breath of Ram. Give me strength, intelligence, and wisdom—Bala Buddhi Vidya Dehu Mohin.

The Chaleesa is filled with phrases that describe Hanuman's attributes, which are sung to remind him of his greatness. As the Chaleesa reminds Hanuman of his greatness, so are we reminded of our greatness—our ability to revisit our highest self.

Devotion opens the door. Hanuman opens the door. By using him as our model and reciting the Hanuman Chaleesa, we become one with that energy. After a while, we find we are in the state of grace, even when we are working or socializing. Before we know it, we realize we can't turn it off. It's always there. That's what this devotional practice is all about: readjusting our vibratory rate so that we can be in a state of love and unity with our highest self all the time, and our actions emanate from that place.

The verses of the Chaleesa are all entrees into the world of devotion:

Any difficult work is made easy by your grace. You are the keeper of Ram's door. Devotion is the guard at the door to pure consciousness.

All happiness comes to those you shelter. With you as their protector, what is there to fear? How can we fear anything when we know in our hearts that we are immortal, that love is perpetually available, and that our consciousness is forever spotless when we are beyond the pulls of our minds?

You are radiant, and the worlds tremble at your roar.

Egoless devotional people are radiant. For example, as difficult as her life was, Mother Theresa had a radiance; she experienced the joy of doing, and history dictates the success of her undertakings.

Ghosts and demons cannot come near when your name is recited, O great brave one.

Reciting the holy names and mantras is the greatest defense against the demons of ego and fear. These vibrations make our minds the servant of Divine will. Diseases are cured and all suffering is removed by unceasing repetition of his name. We can agree that miracles really do occur. Keeping our mind focused with these positive energies has been proven to have the ability to heal.

Your glory fills the four ages. You are the essence of devotion to Ram, always remaining the servant. This is the energy that yearns to serve the One—the yearning of God wanting to return to God is the purpose of devotion. With these practices, we fan the flame of our yearning and remain constant in our goal. Devotion gives all happiness.

Hail Hanuman. Bestow your grace on me as my guru. Teach me how to be perfect in my devotion. Be my teacher.

From his exalted place, he will hear our petitions.

Make your camp in my heart. We keep pure consciousness in the safety of our hearts and take refuge in the miracle of knowing we are all united in that noble cause.

When we get beyond the metaphors of the Chaleesa and have a deeper understanding of the energy it contains, it transforms us forever. By acknowledging the divinity inside, we serve God and become closer and more unified in our love and praise for each other.

Comprehend the enormity of that dynamic. Imagine the power that would be unleashed if everyone in the world consciously loved and praised each other. It's immense! And it's self-perpetuating; it grows and grows. In praising each other, we focus on the joy of living. We elect not to sit in our suffering; we find a way out of our suffering by living in joy. Hanuman is never somber or sad, but he is sober and clear in his determination. That clarity can put an end to our confusion.

We are all magnificent in our souls. We can communicate soul-to-soul and live in a state of peace. Devotional practices may seem new and bizarre to you. However, they are not any stranger than the way we live our lives now. These methods have stood the test of time and have been in use for thousands of years. Try them. You can always return to your old ways or seek another path.

It is all up to us. We are the ones we have been waiting for. We are the elders, and with that honored position comes the serious obligation to serve each other with love, integrity, wisdom, and compassion. With this as the goal of our existence, we can create a world suitable for the gods to inhabit—the gods that exist and thrive within all of us.

After all, all roads lead to Ram: PURE CONSCIOUSNESS.

CHAPTER 35

MANIFESTING A DREAM FOR RAM DASS

BABA RAM DASS was my beloved friend and mentor, and he taught me so much. One of his most remarkable attributes was his ability to maintain an intense focus on an objective. He had always dreamed of introducing Lord Hanuman, the Hindu Monkey God, to America. Accomplishing that was one of the greatest achievements of his very spectacular life.

Hanuman represents the essence of selfless service. As reported in the ancient texts—the Mahabharata, the Puranas, and most importantly, the Ramayana—Hanuman was in fact a manifestation of Lord Shiva, who is part of the Hindu trinity. According to scripture, Lord Shiva heard that Lord Vishnu was going to visit humanity in the form of Sri Rama, to save the goodness of humanity from the destruction of all the negative forces present at the time on Earth. Shiva wanted to help Vishnu with this endeavor, but needed to disguise himself, so he assumed the form of a monkey. But Shiva, being all-powerful himself and not wanting to blow his own cover, did not let Hanuman know the origins of his creation. In this way, Hanuman served with constant humility. His only purpose was to serve Lord Vishnu and ensure that humanity would survive.

This is why we sing the Hanuman Chaleesa: to remind Hanuman of his superpowers, and to petition him to assist and serve us.

But back to Ram Dass. Some fifty years ago, he was on a trip to India, where he met with his guru, Neem Karoli Baba, also known as Maharaji. When Ram Dass returned to the United States, he decided he wanted to introduce his newly acquired philosophy and teachings to America. He wanted to serve our western culture and raise the standards that had seemingly degenerated at that time.

Translated through his academic training and brilliant mind, this wisdom soon captivated many here in the West. This was in the late 1960s and early 1970s, and our minds were hungry for the simplicity of Maharaji's mandates: to love everybody, feed everybody, see God in everybody, and always tell the Truth. As interest in these revelations grew, and particularly after Ram Dass published his groundbreaking book, *Be Here Now,* he became even more concerned with creating a real center for these doctrines in the US. By then, his popularity was rising, and he had established himself as a leader in the Maharaji collective. We all loved him dearly and actively supported his plan to create a center.

Ram Dass commissioned one of the top sculptors in Jaipur to create a murti, an image of Hanuman for the future temple. It was based on a painting by an American devotee, Lakshmi (Christine Tiernan), in which the Monkey God takes flight to help save Sita from the demon king Ravana. As the story goes, Sita was being held hostage by the demon king, and Lord Ram gave his ring to Hanuman to present it to Sita—a sign that her beloved Ram would be coming to the rescue. (I know the painting well, since it hung in my own temple room for thirty-six years before I brought it to its permanent home. But I'm getting ahead of myself.)

There was no official temple yet when the massive statue of Hanuman arrived in New Mexico, so it was given refuge in a makeshift barn on property owned by a generous devotee and student of Maharaji, in Taos. But Ram Dass was on a quest that we all followed, and bit by bit, the barn expanded into a remarkable temple and center. Over the span of forty-five years, and with countless donations and improvements, the Neem Karoli Baba Ashram has become a place for pilgrims from all over the world to congregate and celebrate the teachings and doctrines of Maharaji and Hanuman. And it's a fabulous example of the sacred principles of Vedic architecture.

The temple's dedication was scheduled for July 2019. It was to be a massive event, attended by guests from around the world. But no one knew if Ram Dass would be able to be there. My old friend, who was then living in Hawaii, had suffered a stroke some twenty-two years earlier and was ill and weak, confined to a wheelchair. I knew how much the dedication would mean to him, and I knew how determined he was. In all my years with him, I'd witnessed his fortitude. If he could be there, he would.

Hanuman at home in the newly completed Hanuman Mandir in Taos, New Mexico, at the Neem Karoli Baba Ashram.

Finally, it was announced that he would attend. The murti of Hanuman had been installed in the main entry of the temple and was dressed for the occasion—resplendent in proper and formal attire, awaiting Ram Dass's arrival. And then Ram Dass was wheeled into the space.

A look of profound satisfaction and wonder came over my friend's face. He approached the statue and began to cry tears of joy. The ecstasy that flowed through his whole being was obvious and electrifying for all fifteen hundred people there. He was clearly mesmerized by the magnificence of what had been created and by the fact that here was his dream, in glorious manifestation. We were all humbled by the sight of this man experiencing his own accomplishment. With the help of so many, he had given Hanuman a permanent and fitting home in the United States. His mission had been completed. Thinking about it now still takes my breath away. And it's a moment that has become legendary to all Ram Dass's devotees.

The temple celebration continued for a few more days. And then, one morning, one of Ram Dass's attendants called me. Ram Dass wanted all the people who had cared for him at one point or another to assemble for a photograph—was I on the temple grounds, and could I come to the house for the picture?

Of course, I said yes, though in truth I was a good half an hour away. I made the drive through the desert in twelve minutes. But the picture had already been taken, so I went into the house to look for my friend. He was having some lunch, surrounded by a coterie of quiet, reserved people. Many tended to be this way in his presence, but not me. We had always been like brothers, like family, and had been through so much together. I greeted him as I always did, with love, familiarity, and a little razzing:

"So, Baba. I see you are enjoying some repast."

He looked at me with an eyebrow raised, just slightly.

"I have come to be with you for some primetime. And I have something for you," I said. I had brought a bound galley of this book, which was then nearing completion—it wasn't a temple, but it was a dream nonetheless, and one which Ram Dass had supported from early on. Not many people had seen the book yet, but I wanted to make sure he did.

He motioned for me to present it to him, and I did.

He held it in his hand and looked at the cover. He read the subtitle aloud—"The Personal History of a Spiritual Adventurer"—and took a moment, as if considering it. He looked up at me. "Yes, Sruti Ram, it is true. Well done," he said.

He beckoned me to come over, then called for the photographer to return, and requested he take a photograph: Ram Dass, holding up my book, with me standing right next to him. That photo was, and is, an incredible gift.

Ram Dass was the first person to endorse the book, some ten years before anyone else did. He understood more than anyone else the journey I had to take in order to write it. Life had gotten in the way more than once, and set me on detours, but now, as I stood next to him in that house in New Mexico, I felt as if I'd come full circle: from the book's beginnings to its completion, and then to Ram Dass's final approval. I was ecstatic, and near tears. And a sense of gravity, of finality, and of peace filled my psyche. The rest of the time at the temple, we were both light, and filled with joy. And we enjoyed each other's company immensely. We were two men who had each pursued a dream—for each of us it had taken years, and we had made it.

It wasn't the last time I would speak to Ram Dass. But it was the last time I would see him.

In July 2019, at the celebration of the opening of the Neem Karoli Baba Hanuman Mandir in Taos, New Mexico, Sruti Ram presented Ram Dass with an early version of this book.

CHAPTER 36

LEARNING TO RECEIVE: THE LAST CALL

MONTHS HAD PASSED since the Neem Karoli Baba Hanuman Mandir dedication. I was back at home in the Catskill Mountains, and I'd settled back into my routine. And then, one day, what started out as a typical day proved to be anything but.

In my temple, while organizing and performing my daily rituals, I went into a deep meditation. For me, this practice is always the best part of the day.

Sitting quietly, I journeyed to a space within that I didn't recognize. I'd never seen it before. There was a dark circular chamber, and all around its perimeter were entrances to mysterious hallways. One of the entrances glowed with a warm, inviting light, so that's the one I entered.

The hallway led me to a gigantic door. As I opened the door, it fell down and became a bridge, so I started to cross it. When a path opens for you like this, take it, as you never know what wonders it may lead you to. At the end of the bridge, I reached a magnificent golden throne. How wonderful!

I took my place on the throne and continued to meditate. Suddenly, I was inundated with enormous, electric energy. It was almost overwhelming, but I wasn't frightened at all. I stayed open, totally accepting. Soon it became clear what I was experiencing: love energy. LOVE. It was the culmination of all the love of a lifetime, flooding me all at once.

It was glorious. But soon I had a realization: I had some ego about all of this Love. All the love I had experienced in my life was filtered through my understanding that it was *my* ability to love that generated this enormous energy. I'd misunderstood this power all these years. Instead of accepting it, I was controlling it. I was trying to draw it toward me, to tend to the others who loved me, to love them *more*—and I had been taking all the credit.

That's why I was there. Finally, I was able to remove my ego. I was able to detach it, to unhook it, in a sense, and to allow the spectacular flow of love emanating from the world and universe to enter my consciousness with the crystal clarity of its source.

WOW.

The revelation literally blew me away. It blew my ego out of the picture.

To acknowledge that I had been taking credit for all the love in my life was an enormous revelation. To think that I was the creator of all this divine energy was so wrong. No, the truth was this: I was unmistakably loved. I was *being* loved. And that I could be loved so totally and so truly was the culmination of my lifetime of searching and yearning. I had tapped into the divine source of creation, my birthright. And I knew it.

Thank God. And I do, every day.

Of course, I wanted to call Ram Dass and tell him all about this. On the phone, he sounded weak, but he was very present with me, as always. He consistently stayed in the present moment.

"Baba," I said excitedly, "I have had the most incredible experience, and I want to tell you all about it!"

"Well, what happened?"

I related all the details: the usual meditation ritual in my own temple, the hallway and the bridge, the throne, and then the LOVE, followed by the realization that my own ego was getting in the way. I told him how I was able to remove it and then felt a tidal wave of clarity and joy.

Ram Dass was quiet on the phone, just listening.

"What do you think about it?" I asked him.

"Great," he said. "You have accomplished the ability to RECEIVE."

He was right, of course, and I said so. And then I asked him: "Anything else to say about it?" It was a seeker's query, a student's query, an old friend consulting with another, a question based on years of trust. I was so open to receive right then in a way I hadn't been in so long.

He seemed to be considering my question. And then he answered me. "I only have one thing more to say about it," he said in his quiet voice. "Sruti Ram, I love you. I love you. I love you. I LOVE you. I love YOU." He repeated it again and again, with such sweetness, about twenty times. And then gently, he hung up the phone.

That was the last time I spoke to Ram Dass. My marvelous ally, my friend left his body about five days later.

I shall never forget that phone call with him. And I will always be eternally grateful to him for his guidance and interpretation. You see, he was all about LOVE. That was his life's journey: the path of love and truth. He talked the talk and walked the walk, in front of the entire world.

RAM RAM.

CONCLUSION

D EVOTIONAL LOVE IS an exquisite energy that rises above the usual ego-motivated ideas based on our desires. It is directly connected to a power of exceptional recognition of the higher self. We transform ourselves and establish our ability to see and experience the profoundly evolved characteristics of people and life.

Through a spiritual practice of loving a form of the Divine, we evolve to a higher level of consciousness. We acknowledge the potential and majesty of a greater power in our lives and strive to accommodate that power for the simple joy of doing so. In the process of serving that higher power, we are changed. The more real our devotion is, the faster our evolution. We begin to realize the profound effect of devotion, and ultimately, this energy prioritizes our entire existence. The whole process is a kind of surrender: a realization, if you will, that an unseen force is most definitely in control.

In some instances, the rational mind will battle and try to return us to our old egocentric ways. By denying the truth and choosing not to surrender, we attempt to maintain the belief that we are in control. The practice of devotional love changes that attitude. Slowly, the process of dedicating all our actions to the divine form we have chosen establishes the knowledge of a higher purpose for our incarnation—to enhance the work that leads towards our perfection.

By letting go of our plans, we create space for divine intervention in our lives. We begin to recognize the divine attributes and celebrate that cognition. We begin to gravitate towards people and situations in which we see and feel the presence of these attributes.

All actions are determined by thought. The function of devotional practice is to evolve to a place where we actually reverse negative and destructive thought patterns. Love becomes a constant practice, and love of God directs the mind to positive energy. Embracing this method enables us to dissociate from destructive thought patterns, and success—a new level of joy and even bliss—is guaranteed. We experience internal peace even in the midst of worldly turmoil.

Consciousness is prior to thought. Once we get to know love through devotional practice, a higher consciousness is created and from this Divine Consciousness comes all thought and form. The Divine supports all—everything. Devotional love helps us to forget ourselves and center on the Divine. Devotion purifies the mind and ultimately promotes selfless service to humanity. When we leave the consciousness of being the body, we enter the heart space where peace and noble thoughts originate.

Through the practice of devotional love, worldly illusions become less and less important, and ultimately, we merge into a state of consciousness where we know that God is closer than we ever believed possible.

We can do it, but we must want it. We must make the effort. Once we attain that heart space created by devotional love, we are changed from the individual ego to a universal consciousness, and we never return completely to the state of the suffering ego. We become the master and are released from bondage. We *become* the essence that we once practiced adoring.

Ram Ram.

REMEMBRANCES

Sruti Ram in 2020, the year of his passing.

YOU DON'T HAVE TO
BE AFRAID TO LOVE

I first met Sruti Ram at a Ram Dass retreat in Rhode Island in 1976. After being blown away by Ram Dass at a lecture in Washington, DC, two years earlier, I had bought tapes of his retreats, and I'd been dreaming and scheming to actually be able to participate in one.

Sruti Ram was the meditation master—and he took his job seriously. At the very first 3:00 a.m. meditation, he had three hundred groggy attendees sitting absolutely still and silent and following their breath. About forty-five minutes into the hour-long sitting, he spoke: "If your legs are asleep, if your back is really hurting, if you absolutely *have* to move—DON'T!"

Now, I had been through seventeen years of Catholic school, including four years of seminary, but I thought, "Wow, this guy's tough." Yet there was an aura about him that drew me to him in a heart-aching way.

The next day, I got in line to talk with Sruti Ram after one of Ram Dass's sessions. I wasn't sure what I wanted to ask or say. After waiting for him to finish conversing with several other retreatants, I finally stood in front of him. He looked at me—and through me—and said, "You know, you don't have to be afraid to love." Then he hauled off and punched me hard in the center of my chest. I fell back like I was at a revival; some people caught me, and I eventually stumbled back to my seat and made it through the rest of the day's program.

The day after that, I got in line again. I wanted to know who my guru was—could Sruti Ram tell me? I was hoping he'd tell me Neem Karoli Baba or Sai Baba or Ramakrishna or Nityananda, but he looked into my eyes and said, "JC, you fool!" Apparently, he could see Christ energy all around me even though I'd rejected the Catholic thing years before. (Years later, Neem Karoli Baba made it very clear to me that he is, in fact, my satguru, but that it had been very important for me to reconnect with Christ before I could move forward.)

Immediately after the retreat, I drove my van back to northwest Arkansas, where I'd been back-to-the-landing it—and packed up

From left: Sruti Ram, Ram Dass, and Vayudas at Omega Institute in the 1980s.

and moved to New York City. Sruti Ram had said maybe I could move into a house of Ram Dass students that he was going to run. I ended up staying with him for more than twenty years.

I was just this guy who'd quit the seminary, gotten married, had a daughter, gotten divorced, turned into a hippie, rediscovered spirituality by way of psychedelics, and become a "seeker." Sruti Ram had some of that in common with me, but the difference was that he *knew*. He knew peoples' hearts, their motivations, their stuck places—and if they were ready, and if they asked, he'd work with them at a deeper level than I'd ever seen or experienced. He could look at someone and know their past lives and what their work was this time around and what next step they needed to take. And, as the situation warranted, he could push them seemingly without mercy, or console them with heartfelt caring. Or both. Either way, his purpose was to move his students forward in their spiritual growth— and he was really good at it.

Living in Sruti Ram's world was never easy, but it was a privilege of the highest order. His extraordinary view of the universe brought him ecstasy and pain—the richness of loving communion and, in equal measure, the pain of stark aloneness. Sometimes, he would go into a trancelike state and receive teachings from other realms. In searching through my papers trying to figure out what to write here, I found this transmission he said was for me; I am humbly sharing it in his honor, because it feels universal:

> Freedom lies precisely in surrender, in willingness to relinquish the hard-won personality—the image of who we are in the world and what we should be—the ego. If we are willing to travel this far, to expect nothing, then nothing can go wrong—no solutions. There is no technique. We are as gods. Whatever happens, happens. This

is a state of surrender, of not trying. For we are now willing to lose everything and find nothing. All that has maintained us in the ordinary world is of no use here. That which was veiled is unveiled. That which was hidden is revealed. Beneath all appearance, beyond all customary distinctions, there is a deeper self that wears no mask. In love we have found nothing and all things. Love is a healing force in a dangerous world. It connects us with other souls and with all the earth—and perhaps with the stars as well.

May your light shine on forever, Sruti Ram!

—ALLAN VICKERS (VAYUDAS)

OM NAMAH SHIVAYA

Sruti Ram was more fully, completely, unapologetically himself than almost anyone I have known. He was a magical wizard of a human being with the presence of a mountain, the temperament of a diva, the wisdom and mischief and authority of a true yogi. His passion for God was unwavering. He awakened that passion in me when I was very young.

It was the spring of 1976. I had just turned fifteen and left my family in Taos, New Mexico, to follow Ram Dass to New York City with the expectation of becoming enlightened. We all harbored such hopes in that magical era.

Sruti's reputation preceded him. My traveling companions had met him at a Ram Dass retreat at Lama Foundation the summer before and they couldn't stop talking about him, as if he were some combination of awakened master and rock star. I remember waiting my turn in the living room of the house where Sruti presided over a group of seekers and finally being summoned to his room in the basement. He was sitting in half lotus on the floor in front of an elaborate altar overflowing with brightly colored pictures of Indian gods and goddesses, photographs of saints and masters, statues of the Divine Mother and the Buddha, multiple sticks of incense burning at once, and at least a dozen candles flickering. He was holding a mala of fat rudraksha beads with which he silently gestured for me to sit before him. I sat.

Seemingly casually, Sruti flicked his beads at me, grazing my knee. I stared into his eyes. He thumped me again, a little harder. I held his gaze. Then he lifted his hand and pressed his mala hard against the crown of my head. My eyes closed and I lost all sense of spatial relations. I could no longer feel the edges of my body and heard only the sound of my breath rippling like water along a riverbed. And Sruti began to chant. *Om Namah Shivaya*. After what felt like a year, he spoke. "Okay, we're done." He chuckled and I left.

This was the height of the period Sruti describes in this book, in which his spiritual powers were flourishing. Thank God he realized what was happening, the dazzling fruit being offered at a price that would have cost him not only his humanity but probably caused harm to those who fell under his spell. Not because of ill intent. Sruti only wanted liberation for himself and everyone else. But because that role is so seductive and the power differential so imbalanced that it comes trailed by a shadow equal to the light.

Soon afterwards, my companions and I left New York. Ram Dass left too, and the communal houses dissolved. I did not see Sruti Ram again for many years, though he continued to occupy a secret and magical shrine in my heart. Then one day he appeared at the Neem Karoli Baba Ashram in Taos. This was my community. I sang kirtan here, raised my children among the other ashram kids, served in the gift shop during festivals. I did not recognize Sruti at first. The slender man with the sunken cheeks and wild brown hair had metamorphosed into a middle-aged hairdresser from the Bronx with a silver ponytail and trendy eyeglasses. He was unpretentious, if a bit eccentric, and when I reminded him of our encounter twenty years earlier, he looked amused. Then he offered to cut my hair.

For the next few years, Sruti Ram visited Taos often and always gave me a haircut beneath the apple tree on the ashram lawn. I knew it was more than a haircut and that Sruti was more than a stylist. He was working with my energy, sharing shakti, doing his wild Sruti dance with my soul. But it was grounded and integrated now, less dramatic and more human. Also more equal. We met as two old friends on the path. It's just that one of us had hairstyling skills the other didn't. And a particular gift for channeling light in such a way that the other person's heart lit up.

Over the last few years of his life, Sruti Ram sent me Facebook messages on a regular basis. "Ram Ram. Hi darlin', thinking about you today. Hope all is well out there for you and yours. Take care and be safe. Ram Ram." Or "Ram Ram dearest. Keep spreading the light." And, when I was doubting my ability to hold any kind of spiritual leadership in this world, he advised me, "Come from your beautiful golden heart, be there for a moment—leave your mind behind—proceed to be Mirabai, who loved Krishna more than anything. Like Siddhi Ma said to me, 'Remember the feeling, then share it with others.' Love you, dearest."

This was our last exchange. Me: "How are you faring?" Sruti: "Good enough for an old fart." Me: "Haha. You'll always be a rock star to me." Sruti: "And you are a rock. Take care, beloved, and keep safe."

These missives were shots of energy and love that always showed up when I needed them most. I had a feeling I was not the only recipient of Sruti Ram's thoughtful, generous, loving outreach. He watered many gardens with his abundant heart. I miss him.

— MIRABAI STARR

"TRICKED"

I met Sruti Ram at a home kirtan gathering. These gatherings encompassed a community of spiritual seekers from a variety of Indian paths with various gurus and belief systems. I had recently moved to the Hudson Valley and had been invited to the kirtan by Shyamdas. I had just finished setting up a recording studio and wanted to record some of the singers at the kirtan. I happened to sit next to Sruti Ram and heard his exquisite voice harmonizing with the other singers. That night I mentioned recording to him. He seemed agreeable, but it would take a year of prodding before it was done.

Over time, I came to know that it was Neem Karoli Baba's desire for Sruti Ram to record a CD. *Sruti Ram and the Mirabai Chorus* was made live with too many instruments and singers. I had placed microphones in various spots in the room, and when I listened to them separately, I heard offkey singing and noticed some other production difficulties. I told Neem Karoli Baba that it was up to him to get this record made.

Sruti Ram came by one day to hear what I had done. I had never told him that I was a singer, but that day, I mentioned that I had studied opera. He, too, had studied opera. We both knew "Ave Maria," so we launched into a version, with him harmonizing with me. It was otherworldly. It was the beginning of something.

We both knew Neem Karoli Baba had "tricked" us into this situation.

It was a divine pairing. With my alto and his tenor, we created haunting melodies that had us traveling the universe through song. We were both passionate about chanting the glories of the Divine Names. It never really mattered if anyone else liked it because we were enjoying ourselves too much. We released three CDs. The first one, *Fire of Devotion*, we recorded as Sruti Ram & Ishwari; then we shortened our name to SRI Kirtan and released *Live Your Love* and *Time in Love Is Never Wasted*.

I am grateful to have listened to the call. I feel complete in what we have left in this world together. I will miss the supportive and powerful voice and the energized *kartal* (hand bells) playing that were Sruti Ram's signature.

——ISHWARI L. KELLER

Sruti Ram and Ishwari (SRI Kirtan).

MY DEAR SRUTI RAM

Sruti Ram had the most zeal for life of anyone I've ever known. When I met him over dinner in 2013, it was more than forty years since he had been a teacher of Hinduism in Richmond Hills, New York. Yet, it was clear that I had encountered a man imbued with an extraordinary sense of life—a real force of nature. His zeal for life was immediately evident in his disarming smile, his laugh, the joy he showed almost everyone he met.

In the seven years I knew Sruti Ram, I saw him manifest wonder, magic, and joy in every aspect of his life. I was moved by his reverence and sincerity during daily puja and his worship of his murtis—chanting over them, lighting incense, ringing a bell. He often spent more than an hour a day chanting, accompanying himself on his harmonium. He also meticulously sewed beautiful garments for his murtis, changing their dress often throughout the year. Though I didn't share Sruti Ram's faith, I was moved by his commitment to his practice, and I took it to heart when he invited me to join him in observation, meditation, and chant. When he led kirtan, I loved his lyrical, Jim Morrison-style voice, how he moved his shoulders and swayed while playing the finger cymbals—he was ecstatic.

At home, he manifested a sense of magic and wonder too. Decorated eclectically, his house holds not only Hindu deities, but also lovely sculptures, crystal plates, Tiffany lamps, and contemporary art and furniture. When guests came to visit, he illuminated the entire house with real and remote-controlled candles, his many lamps, and even colored glass-bedecked peacocks and blinking avatar trees.

Sruti Ram's commitment to being engaged IN life was demonstrated daily through his focused completion of the tasks of living: with his body aching, he'd blow leaves or shovel snow for two hours; if a window blind or audio machine or vacuum broke, he'd spend hours figuring out how to fix it; if, after shopping for groceries, he found that a cabinet was too small to hold everything, he'd rearrange its contents so that everything fit perfectly. He put his full attention to whatever task was at hand until it was resolved.

But he also had a childlike spirit, charmingly spontaneous. He'd create his own languages and engage in conversations using them.

Sruti Ram and Jonathan Dobin attending Ishwari Keller's wedding.

He'd suddenly improvise operatic-styled arias in a ringing helden-tenor voice.

His personal integrity was an example for me to follow. He stood firm about who he was; no matter the circumstances, he was always his most authentic self. He wasn't afraid to stand up against what he thought was an affront. I was amazed by the friendship and warmth he showed each person with whom he interacted. He gave heartfelt greetings to everyone he knew—and when Sruti Ram spoke to you, it was as if you were the only person who mattered in the entire world. How heart-enriching and joyful!

I was fifty-eight years old when I met Sruti Ram, and I'd had a lifetime of accomplishments, losses, pain, and searching for love. I knew I'd discovered a soul-friend. Other than perhaps with my mother and father, I have never felt more loved, more at home, more secure, more valued and cherished, and more SEEN as the man I am—with all my fears, insecurities, and strengths—in my LIFE than I did with Sruti Ram. How grateful I am to have come into his life, and that he shared with me, so fully, generously, and completely, who he was: vulnerable, strong, loving, playful, serious—a complex man. How blessed I have been for his love.

—JONATHAN DOBIN

A PLACE IN MY HEART

I met Sruti Ram in the late 1990s at our mutual friend Shyamdas's house in upstate New York on Janmastami, the celebration of the Appearance of Sri Krishna. I had known Shyamdas since the 70s when I lived in Vrindavan, India, Lord Krishna's birthplace, but we hadn't seen each other in decades. When I heard Shyamdas had moved upstate, where I'd been living since 1993, I called him, and he invited me over for Janmashtami.

I didn't know anyone but Shyam, but soon a friendly man started talking to me. It was Sruti Ram. When I told him that I had been practicing bhakti yoga since the mid-60s and how I wished there was kirtan in the area, he said that actually kirtan had been going on upstate for decades, at his house, every Tuesday night! I was very happy to hear that.

So, I started attending Sruti Ram's wonderful home kirtans. They were quite small at first, just a few people, but they gradually grew to twenty to thirty people. Mainly Sruti, Vayu, and Jonji led the chants, but eventually Jonji talked Sruti into letting me and others lead as well. Sruti played the kartals, and very well. (He was not yet playing the harmonium.) I also was a kartal player, from way back. Sruti was impressed with my large kartals made from bell metal.

When Chetan Jyoti Ma, a wonderful kirtan singer, Krishna

devotee, and renunciate who had been living in Rishikesh for around thirty years, came to visit upstate New York, Sruti put her up at his house. I remember when she and Sruti sang a new version of Sita-Ram, which they had collaborated on. Sruti led the chant for quite a while, and then she led it. It was beautiful, Sruti's best-known chant, which he sang for the rest of his life.

In 2003, I traveled to India. I'd heard that Sruti would be there, but I didn't know quite where or when. Eventually, I went to Vrindavan, a very holy place with over five thousand temples, and cows, monkeys, peacocks, buffaloes, and camels all sharing the streets with thousands of visiting sadhus. The night I arrived, I was heading upstairs to the restaurant connected to the guesthouse where I was staying, and I heard someone coming down the stairs say, "Arundhati?" At first, I couldn't see him in the dim light, but it was Sruti!

I couldn't believe it was him, and he said he thought he had seen a ghost. We were so happy to meet up with each other in that holy place. We hugged, and it was just so amazing. He invited me to have lunch with him the next day at Neem Karoli Baba Ashram in Vrindavan, where he was staying. I went, and later that day I led a kirtan there, and Sruti introduced me to Siddhi Ma. Then he came to see me, and I brought him to the Krishna Balaram Mandir and other places.

In 2004, we were both in India again and spent some wonderful time together, once more unplanned, in Vrindavan and Rishikesh with Chetan Jyoti Ma, Prema, and Vayu. I took him to Radha-Damodar Mandir, a very sacred spot in Vrindavan, where my guru lived long ago. We walked the *parikrama*, circling the temple complex, and Sruti got so high he was spinning from all the energy there.

When Sruti decided to make the CD *In Divine Love*, a very simple and pure collection of chants, he asked me to sing on it. I led the kirtan "Radhe Radhe Govinda." A few years later, I made my own CD, *Radha-Krishna Journey of Love*. Sruti loved it and was very encouraging.

Throughout the years, chanting was our main connection. We had regular kirtans publicly in Woodstock every Monday night at the bookstore Mirabai, then at Namaste Yoga and Woodstock Yoga. For several years, we held Bhajan boat rides, started by Shyamdas. At first, the main chanters were Shyamdas, SRI Kirtan (Sruti and Ishwari), and me; later, others also led, and there were about a hundred attendees. It was pure ecstasy, sailing, chanting, and dancing down the Hudson River.

Sruti Ram was a special person in my life. Our spiritual paths had some differences, but that was okay. We connected on a heart level. He appreciated my kirtan singing and bhakti path and let me know that repeatedly. We had both been practicing for many decades, so there was a mutual appreciation. He will always have a place in my heart.

— ARUNDHATI DEVI SHERBOW

GLOSSARY

Arti: Hindu ritual of waving a flaming lamp in front of a sacred image.

Ashram: Hindu monastery.

Baba: Father or teacher.

Bhakti: Devotional practice.

Bhavan: A spiritual residence for travelers.

Chai walla: A person who sells hot tea on the streets of India.

Chaleesa: A prayer or hymn of forty verses.

Dalai Lama: His Holiness the Buddhist devotional leader of the Tibetan people.

Devotee: The spiritual practitioner of a specific philosophy.

Dharma: The philosophical law of righteous living.

Durga: A manifestation of Divine Feminine.

Ganesh: Hindu deity, the son of Lord Shiva.

Ganga: A nickname for The Ganges River.

Ghat: A public docking and bathing place on the shore of a river.

Guru: One's teacher.

Hanuman: The manifestation of Lord Shiva and the pinnacle of selfless service.

Hari Om: An expression of Divine Oneness.

Harmonium: Musical keyboard used in kirtan or chanting.

Infinite Correlation: The harmonious merging of universal energies.

Jai: "Hail to," in Hindi.

Jao: "Go" or the command to leave, in Hindi.

Japa: Repetition of a mantra or sacred words, using mala beads, to clear the mind.

Kali: Manifestation of the Divine Feminine.

Karma: The sum of a person's actions in this and past existences, which decides one's fate in future existences.

Kirtan: Method of call-and-response chanting.

Krishna: The human incarnation of Lord Vishnu.

Laxman: Brother of Lord Ram.

Lord Ram: The incarnation of Lord Vishnu before Krishna.

Lord Ramachandra: Another name for Lord Ram.

Lord Vishnu: Part of the Hindu godhead trinity.

Maharani: Princess or queen.

Maharishi: Term used to describe one's highest teacher.

Mandir: Temple.

Mantra: Sacred word used to induce spiritual states.

Meenakshi: A manifestation of sacred feminine.

Murti: A sacred image, usually fabricated in metal, stone, or wood.

Namaste: "I honor the God within you."

Om: The sound made when the universe was created.

Prasad: Blessed food offered to the gods, then consumed by practitioners.

Puja: Hindu ritual.

Raksha Bandhan: Hindu festival honoring brothers, sisters, and friends.

Ram Dass (1931-2019): American philosopher, spiritual teacher, and leader.

Ramayana: The epic story written about the trials and tribulations of Lord Ram.

Rishis: Highly respected and knowledgeable teachers and scribes.

Sangha: A spiritual gathering of like-minded people.

Sari: A garment worn by an Indian woman.

Sat Guru: A person's highest teacher.

Satsang: A spiritual gathering of like-minded people.

Seva: Service to others.

Shiva: The third member of Hindu trinity.

Siddhis: Yogic powers.

Sita: Lord Ram's consort.

Sri: Title of great respect.

Sruti: Another name for an Upanishad: the revealed word of God; in music, the sound between the notes.

Swami: Hindu priest.

Swarup: An image that is a direct manifestation of God.

Thakurji: A worshiped, sacred image.

Tilak: A mark drawn and worn on the forehead.

Upa Guru: A spiritual teacher

Upanishad: Wisdom handed down orally through the centuries.

Vastu: The scientific study of placement of articles to enhance the flow of energy.

Vrindavan's Loi Bazar: Main shopping center in the city of Vrindavan.

Yatra: A sacred journey or pilgrimage.

Yogi: A practitioner of yoga.

Yogiraj: One who has mastered a specific practice of yoga.

ACKNOWLEDGMENTS

Thanks to my dear friend, the late Baba Ram Dass, who so generously shared his wisdom and support. As I made an indestructible commitment to this life and practice, he played a profoundly important role.

The creation of this book had many influences, starting with my mother, Mrs. Rose Palmer, who instilled in me a sense of righteousness and courage. She was a devout Catholic, and her life was a clear marker on the path to devotion and authentic practice.

As I matured and began to explore which spiritual philosophies to embrace, I gradually moved toward Hinduism and encountered the Sanskrit Vedas and the Ramayana, for which I am eternally grateful.

Heartfelt thanks also go to my teachers: Hilda Charlton, Sathya Sai Baba, Baba Muktananda, Yogi Dinkar, Swami Gopal Ananda Ghiri, and Swami Nardananda.

My colleagues on this journey—Vayu Vickers, Cheytan Jyoti Ma, and Shyam Das—gave me support and living knowledge to escort me on this spiritual path.

Immense gratitude to Baba Neem Karoli—the discovery that he had chosen me to be one of his devotees altered the very course of my life; and to Siddhi Ma. They remind us that we are all so much more than we could ever think we are.

I wish to thank Dr. Stephan Rechtschaffen, Sharon Gannon, and Ramananda John E. Welshons, Krishna Das, Daniel Goleman, and Elizabeth Lesser for their generous endorsements. And finally, thanks to Jana Martin, Nina Shengold, Sherrie McCain, and Jonathan Dobin for their unwavering support and encouragement in completing this project, which has added to the wonder of this book. Each has fed my spirit and heart with compassionate love and guidance.

We are all Divine and we are all One.

For Sruti Ram, elegance came naturally.